The 17-Inch Baseball Bat

A Baseball Legend

by

Charles M. Province

Copyright © 2021 by Charles M. Province

All Rights Reserved.

Books by Charles M. Province

Helen
Pure Patton
Patton's Proverbs
The Story of Helen
Patton's Third Army
Patton's Punch Cards
The Unknown Patton
I Was Patton's Doctor
Japanese Assault Boats
General Patton's Medals
The 17-Inch Baseball Bat
Ten Twisted Tawdry Tales
The Blood-Stained Benders
A Long Way From Flat River
Patton's One-Minute Messages
The Mine Shaft in My Backyard
Adventures of the Flat River Kid
A Little Kid From Flat River (Vol. 1)
A Little Kid From Flat River (Vol. 2)
A Little Kid From Flat River (Vol. 3)
A Little Kid From Flat River (Vol. 4)
General Walton Walker; Forgotten Hero
A Message to Garcia; The Complete Story
Tail-gunner: The Leonard E. Thompson Story
Patton's Third Army in WWII (Juvenile Edition)

Books Edited by Charles M. Province

Ben Hogan Says . . .
Saber Exercise, 1914
A Living History of Flat River, Missouri
Generalship; It's Diseases and Their Cure
A History of the St. Joseph Lead Company
The Lead Belt News; Tours of the St. Joe Mines

CMP Publishing House
Email: cmprovince@gmail.com
Website: www.pattonhq.com/cmp.html

ST. LOUIS BROWNS

SPORTSMAN'S PARK • 2911 N. GRAND BLVD. • ST. LOUIS 7, MISSOURI • TELEPHONE: LUcas 3385

Table of Contents

Chapter One:
A Sportsman's Park Double-Header..........................1

Chapter Two:
Sportsman's Park; A Thumbnail History..............12

Chapter Three:
A Game To Be Remembered...19
    A Summary of the complete game.....................52

Chapter Four:
The Cast Of Characters...62
    Bill Veeck...62
    Eddie Gaedel..88
    Bob Cain...128
    Bob Swift..134
    Jim Delsing..138
    Frank Saucier..142
    Zack Taylor..148

Chapter Five:
Midgets of Note: Baseball & Otherwise...............152
    Jerry D. Sullivan..154
    Larry Tattersall..175
    Edmond Ansley..181
    Billy Barty...182
    Johnny Roventini..183
    Max Bournstein...184

The 17-Inch Baseball Bat

Chapter One

A Sportsman's Park Double-Header.

It was a normal, humid Missouri day in Flat River when my Uncle Bud drove up in front of Grandma's house. He was Mama's brother and he was there to pick me up and drive me to Aunt Theresa's house in the south-side of St. Louis. She lived just a few blocks away from the Anheuser-Busch brewery. At that time, the brewery was also where the company kept (and spoiled) the company's stunningly beautiful Clydesdale horses, long before the Busch family built Busch Gardens in Williamsburg, Virginia. My cousin, Mary, and I used to occasionally walk down to the brewery's stables to watch the horses as they were being exercised and trained. I'll never forget the delicious aroma covering the neighborhood as Budweiser beer was being brewed on a soft, warm spring day.

Mama was ill once more and in the hospital. That meant that I would, once again, be sent off to spend time with Aunt Theresa and her family; Uncle Herman and their daughter Mary. I don't know why my brother, Harold, was always

The 17-Inch Baseball Bat

allowed to stay with my grandparents and I was the one always chosen to "visit" relatives for a short time. I must have been a troublesome handful, I guess. I really didn't care, though, I got along quite well with all of my aunts, uncles, and cousins. I'm sure it was as much of a welcome holiday for me as it was for Grandma Province.

As usual, I had no idea where my old man was. During those periods when Mama suffered from her bouts with the kidney disease that eventually killed her, I hardly ever saw him. I had grown used to the idea of him living his own life.

Being a healthy six-year-old boy, I was quite resilient, however. I bounced when I fell, I healed quickly from bumps and bruises, and I was naïve enough to believe that the grownups always did what was in my best interest. I never questioned why Uncle Bud was the one driving me to St. Louis, I just figured the old man must be busy doing something else. Besides, I liked Uncle Bud and he seemed to like me. He often told me funny stories about his army days during World War II, serving in various supply depots in the Pacific Theater.

In spite of the situation, August 19, 1951 turned out to be quite a day for me; a small, six-

The 17-Inch Baseball Bat

year-old boy who was already used to being shuttled around and taken care of by grandparents as well as aunts and uncles on occasion.

To be honest, I don't remember a whole lot about the things that occurred at Sportsman's Park that day, but I do remember the truly important things. I have those snapshot images firmly filed away in my "video repository" and I occasionally replay them in my head . . . and it always makes me smile.

Uncle Bud was a big-time baseball fan and he had decided that since he had to drop me off at Aunt Theresa's, he might just as well make the trip worth his while. That day, Bill Veeck's sorrowful St. Louis Browns baseball team was hosting the Detroit Tigers in a double-header. Since it was a double-header, he figured we could leave Flat River around 8 or 9 o'clock in the morning and we would have plenty of time to drive up the old, high-crowned, two-lane macadam road that linked the Lead Belt area to the giant metropolis of St. Louis, Missouri. In spite of St. Louis being only about 70 miles away, the trip took almost three hours because of the thumpity, twisty-turny road. Missouri, at the time, didn't have the sort of multi-lane, high-speed highways we have today.

Anyway, Uncle Bud figured we could take our time, make our way to Sportsman's Park, watch the last of the first game, enjoy one of Bill Veeck's entertaining "between games" shows, and then watch the entire second game before

The 17-Inch Baseball Bat

he dropped me off at Aunt Theresa's place. By that time, he'd be more than ready to take a leisurely return trip back down the highway to Flat River.

What brought all of these memories into play was something I found as I was rummaging through some old boxes I was planning on getting rid of.

Getting rid of "stuff" is just the sort of thing an old man like me does when he's working through the fourth quarter-century of his life. Luckily, instead of just tossing the boxes out, I sat down and began to dig through them to see if I had anything that might be worth millions of dollars; perhaps a first edition, mint copy of Superman #1 (chuckle, chuckle).

Of course, I never found anything like that, unless one can count faded memories as being worth anything. What I did find, however, was a little box that had been stored away for decades. Inside that box were two tiny bottles; miniature Falstaff Beer bottles that were, in reality, salt-and-pepper shakers.

One of Bill Veeck's enticements for that double-header day in 1951 was this set of salt-and-pepper shakers in the form of miniature Falstaff beer bottles. One set was given to every ticket holder as they walked through the gate to

The 17-Inch Baseball Bat

Sportsman's Park.

The day was advertised as the 100th anniversary celebration of the Falstaff Brewing company in St. Louis. No one really knew when the brewing company started, so Bill randomly picked the date for handing out miniature beer bottles and it worked well with Veeck's festivities. Falstaff was the biggest sponsor Veeck had for his team—The St. Louis Browns—and he had informed the owners of Falstaff that he would do something spectacular for the celebration. Also included with the price of a ticket was a ticket for a free bottle of beer for legal age imbibers.

Sometimes, however, this sort of thing failed to work out as planned. In 1953, for example, during a game between the Browns and the Yankees at Sportsman's Park, the fans became belligerent and more than rowdy. They began a "beer bottle shower" upon the Yankees and the unfortunate escapade turned into a mini-riot inside the ballpark. From that time on, beer at Sportsman's Park was served to fans in paper cups, poured by the vendors.

I remember giving my little beer bottles to Grandma Province. She put them on display in her kitchen in her house at 9Y Theodore Street in Flat River. She had a large collection of salt-and-pepper shakers, all given to her by her sons, daughters, grandchildren, etc. When I was taking shop class at Flat River High School, I made a large, elaborate set of shadow boxes for her so

The 17-Inch Baseball Bat

she would have a place to display them all. She had items like the beer bottles, Aunt Jemina, a television set, the Eiffel tower, chickens, bulldogs, milk bottles, snowmen, Mr. and Mrs. Santa Claus, cows, pigs, . . . all sorts of miniatures.

I honestly don't even remember how I came to have the Falstaff set. I've tried to figure it out, but I don't remember anyone ever giving them to me. I thought one of my aunts or cousins had taken the entire collection when Grandma died. The universe is replete with such mysteries which will never be solved.

I seem to be rambling. Let's get back to the big game of August 19, 1951.

We finally made our way to Sportsman's Park, Uncle Bud drove by the front entrance to the baseball field and then began to circle the streets surrounding the park, expanding the circle by one block each time until he found a block that had a parking lot. Well, I say parking lot, but it was really somebody's front yard. The owner of the house was letting people park in his driveway and front yard for fifty cents for the entire day.

Uncle Bud asked him, "Are you staying with the cars yourself during the games?"

The guy answered with a strong Italian ac-

The 17-Inch Baseball Bat

cent, "Oh, you betcha, buddy. I'm-a gonna stay on-a my porch. I gotta da base-a-ball-a game on-a da radio so's I know when-a da game she's-a done. Den-a you gotta come-a get-a da car. Hokay, buddy?"

Uncle Bud said, "That sounds great, pal. I'll see you in a few hours."

He handed the guy a dollar bill and said, "Here's a dollar. Keep the change, pal. Just take good care of my car for me."

A big smile spread across the guy's face and he said, "Say! Dat's-a swell, you betcha. I take good-a care for you car, buddy."

Uncle Bud took my hand and we started walking the couple of blocks toward the ballpark. He bought our tickets, we went in, found our seats, and we settled in for the long haul. We were there in time to catch the last inning of the first game

We watched the "between games" festivities, thoroughly enjoyed the incredible, history-making first inning of the second game and by the time the fifth inning was starting, I was fading fast. I kept falling asleep, leaning against Uncle Bud. When the seventh inning began, he shook me awake and said, "Hey, wake up! I think you've had it, kiddo. Let's go get the car and head over the your Aunt Theresa's place."

I staggered to my feet, he took my hand, and we started toward the nearest exit. By the time we were back at the car, I was a lot more awake. Uncle Bud thanked the guy for looking after his

The 17-Inch Baseball Bat

car and we took off. After a couple of minutes, I was out like a light again. I barely remember him carrying me up the steps to Aunt Theresa's house and nothing else after that.

The next thing I knew, it was morning and Aunt Theresa was shaking me awake. I opened my eyes and rolled onto my back. The sunlight was streaming through the attic window, covering the make-shift bed she always fixed up for me when I came to visit.

She said, "Your Uncle Herman's downstairs having breakfast. He wants to see you before he goes to work."

I said, "Yes, Ma'am. I'll be right down."

I got up, put my clothes on headed downstairs.

As I walked into the kitchen Uncle Herman looked up at me, smiled, and he said, "Well, well. Ain't you the lucky little fella? You got to see the Browns make history young man. Look at that there."

He laid the sports section of the St. Louis Post-Dispatch on the plate sitting next to him. On the front page was a picture of a midget standing at home plate with a small bat in his hands and a look of intense concentration on his face.

I said, "Yes, sir! I saw that. Uncle Bud and I thought it was the funniest thing we ever saw."

He said, "Tell ya whut, you keep this paper and when I get home from work we'll go over the whole story and talk about it. I want to hear

The 17-Inch Baseball Bat

everything you can remember, okay?"

I said, "Yes, sir. I've never seen a midget like that before, except for that little guy on Spike Jones' show. He's funny."

"Yeah, I watch him every week, too," said Uncle Herman.

I really liked Uncle Herman. He was always good to me and he treated me like just a regular guy. He used to send me down to the corner tavern with his beer bucket. The bartender would fill it with Stag beer, then he'd say, "I'll put that on your Uncle's tab, pal," and I'd take it back to Uncle Herman who would drink it with his supper. Things were different back then.

With that, Uncle Herman stood up, patted my shoulder, picked up his lunch pail, and headed off to his "fireman" job at the Mallinckrodt Plant. It wasn't until I was much older that I learned the Mallinckrodt Plant was an old potato farm before World War II, but when the plant was built there, it became a huge operation that produced over 50,000 tons of purified uranium on the banks of the Mississippi River.

The Mallinckrodt company supplied all of the purified, enriched uranium for the "Little Boy" and "Fat Man" atomic bombs that were dropped on Hiroshima and Nagasaki, respectively, to end the Pacific War.

When Uncle Herman came home from work, we had supper (Aunt Theresa, Uncle Herman, Mary, and me) and then he and I went to his basement where we discussed the game, espe-

The 17-Inch Baseball Bat

cially the first inning when Eddie Gaedel came up to the plate to pinch-hit for Frank Saucier.

He made me feel really important. He asked me about the game, the crowd, the pre-game show, and everything else about that historical day. He even let me have a couple of sips of his beer, saying, "Don't you dare tell your Aunt Theresa!"

It was a great day.

The game was soon forgotten, we got on with our lives, and a couple of weeks later, I returned to Flat River to start the second grade.

It wasn't until I found the Falstaff salt-and-pepper set that I began to have flashbacks about that day at Sportsman's Park, Uncle Bud, Eddie Gaedel, and all the rest of it.

Then I really got started; digging into the history of the St. Louis Browns Baseball Team in St. Louis, Missouri. I began by referencing what Rudyard Kipling referred to as the "six honest serving men" in his poem in "The Elephant's Child:"

I keep six honest serving men,
(They taught me all I knew);
Their names are What and Why and When,
and How and Where and Who.

To tell the story of Eddie Gaedel and his "17-

The 17-Inch Baseball Bat

Inch Bat" we shall start at the very beginning, continue through the middle, and finish at the end. Since professional baseball needs a ball park in which to play the game, that's where the story shall begin.

The 17-Inch Baseball Bat

Chapter Two

Sportsman's Park;
A Thumbnail History

Sportsman's Park was officially opened on April 23, 1902 at the northwest corner of Grand Boulevard and Dodier Street, on the north side of St. Louis. It was renovated in 1909, and it was expanded in both 1922 and 1926. When the ball park was first constructed, it could handle about 8,000 paying customers but by the time the last game was played in the aging structure, it could handle almost 31,000 fans. It was demolished in 1966.

During the park's career, it was the home of a number of teams; the St. Louis Brown Stockings, the St. Louis Browns, the St. Louis Cardinals, the St. Louis All-Stars (NFL team), the St. Louis Gunners (NFL team), the St. Louis Soccer League, and the St. Louis Cardinals (NFL team).

In an odd twist of fate, there was a team called the St. Louis Brown Stockings in the American Association that played in the park for a year or two. This team faded and the best players were absorbed by the National League, changing the baseball team's name to the Car-

The 17-Inch Baseball Bat

dinals. The team color was also changed, from Brown to Cardinal Red. This new Cardinal team built a ballpark named "New" Sportsman's Park, but it burned to the ground in 1901. A subsequent park was built for the Cardinals while they played the season as "away" games and it was given the name of Robison Field.

By this time, a new American League team had started in St. Louis. The Milwaukee Brewers had moved to St. Louis and adopted the simple, shortened name of the Browns.

By the mid-1920s, the Cardinals grew unhappy with Robison Field, however. They had become the better and more successful of the two St. Louis teams and their old, mostly-wooden bleacher structure had become inadequate.

After discussions and agreements with the Browns owners, the Cardinals moved back to Sportsman's Park and both the Cardinals and the Browns played all of their games there until 1953, when the Browns left town, moved to Baltimore, and became the Baltimore Orioles. Bill Veeck, the final owner of the Browns did not make the move to Baltimore. He had been politically ousted by the majority of American League team owners due to their disapproval of his carefree and cavalier attitudes concerning the game of baseball. He wanted to have fun and make money . . . they were only concerned with the idea of making money.

After almost winning the American League

The 17-Inch Baseball Bat

Pennant in 1922, Phil Ball, the owner of the Browns at that time, bragged that he would guarantee a World Series would be played in St. Louis by 1926. And he was correct in his prediction, with the exception that it wasn't the Browns in the Series; it turned out to be the St. Louis Cardinals playing the New York Yankees. The Cardinals provided a stunning upset for their fans, defeating the Yankees in a highly memorable seventh game. The Cardinals, yet again, had out-classed the Browns.

When Phil had announced his prediction about the 1926 baseball activities, he also put his money where his mouth was, and he expanded the ballpark from a capacity of 18,000 to 30,000 in preparation for his "guaranteed" World Series.

After the Cardinals' win of the 1926 World Series, the "Red Birds" clearly became the favorite baseball organization in St. Louis.

Ironically, due to the shortage of manpower during World War II, it turned out that the St. Louis Cardinals ended up playing against the St. Louis Browns in the 1944 World Series. The Browns did the best they could, but they were unable to usurp the domination of the city's baseball diamond and they lost the Series 4 games to 2.

It proved to be the last World Series played entirely in a single ballpark that was the home venue for both competing teams. It was, however, an extremely popular Series and the news-

The 17-Inch Baseball Bat

papers and radio gave it the moniker of "The Streetcar Series."

It was in 1936 that Phil Ball died and his family sold the St. Louis Browns to a man named Donald Lee Barnes. The family, however, retained the ownership of Sportsman's Park and began to receive rental checks from the Browns baseball team. Finally, the family tired of even that small connection with professional baseball and they agreed to sell Sportsman's Park back to the Browns for a little over one million dollars.

Mr. Barnes, continued to own both the team and the ballpark until 1951; and that is when Bill Veeck purchased 80 percent of the team and became embroiled in the St. Louis baseball scene.

It was Veeck's intention to drive the Cardinals out of the city as he felt that it could not support two professional baseball teams adequately. It turned out that by the 1950s, St. Louis had, indeed, become a one team town, but it was not the Cardinals who would be leaving. In 1953, the Browns left town, moved to Baltimore, and became the Orioles.

Sportsman's Park was demolished in 1966 and replaced by a new baseball field named Busch Stadium. Then, Busch Stadium was demolished and the land was donated to the city by August Busch. It currently is home to a Boys and Girls Club.

The current Busch Stadium was built at 700

The 17-Inch Baseball Bat

Clark Avenue from which can be seen the famous St. Louis Arch, referred to as the "Gateway to the West." When the arch was being built, the Mayor of East St. Louis, across the Mississippi River in Illinois, joked that he was making plans to build a large "Croquet Mallet" opposite the St. Louis Arch, but, luckily, the idea never came to fruition.

The 17-Inch Baseball Bat

Sportsman's Park in St. Louis, Missouri. A perfect example of Bill Veeck's idea of the nighborhood baseball Park. Bill greatly disliked the "multi-use" coliseum type structures.

The 17-Inch Baseball Bat

Sportsman's Park in 1944, during the "Street Car" World Series played between the Browns and the Cardinals. If you couldn't buy a ticket, you could always climb to the roof of the ballpark.

The 17-Inch Baseball Bat

Chapter Three

A Game To Be Remembered!

With his usual fanfare, bluster, and pyrotechnics, on the first night of his ownership of the St. Louis Browns, Bill Veeck gave either a free beer or a free soda to every person in the ballpark.

From the time he took possession of the team, it only took him six weeks to implement his most famous stunt; bringing in a pinch-hitter who was only 3-feet, 7-inches tall; a twenty-six-year-old young man by the name of Eddie Gaedel. It happened on August 19, 1951.

In preparation for the upcoming event, Bill spent a lot of time and energy letting everyone in St. Louis know that 1951 was the 50th Anniversary of both the American League and the Falstaff Brewing Company—the primary sponsor of the Browns baseball team—and with his unceasing bravado, he managed to get a total of 18,369 fans into the ballpark for the day's double-header.

No one knew for certain when the 50th Anniversary of Falstaff—owned by the Griesedieck Brothers—really was, but things like that never bothered Bill. He was of the opinion that it was

The 17-Inch Baseball Bat

never a good idea to let the truth stand in the way of a good story or a good stunt.

"What can I do," he pondered, "that is so spectacular that no one will be able to say they've seen it before?" The answer was obvious. Remembering a story told by John McGraw, he would send a midget up to bat. Yes, most certainly, that should do the trick.

Some folks have reported that the idea originated with a baseball story written for the Saturday Evening post in 1941 by James Thurber; a story called "You Could Look It Up."

According to Veeck, himself, the idea for such an audacious stunt had been percolating in his mind practically his entire life.

As a teenager, young Veeck got to know many of baseball's personalities, including the New York Giants manager, John McGraw. Veeck said all of the credit goes to McGraw for the idea that led to Veeck's greatest stunt of all; his masterpiece as a baseball showman.

As Veeck explains it, "McGraw had a little hunchback he kept around the clubhouse as sort of a good-luck charm. He wasn't a midget, but was sort of a gnome. By the time McGraw got to the stub of the cigar he was smoking while telling the story, McGraw would swear to my father, Bill, Sr., that one day before he retired, he was going to send his gnome up to bat."

Although McGraw never made good on his promise, Veeck loved the idea and he swore he would, one day, send his own diminutive batter

The 17-Inch Baseball Bat

to the plate.

When Veeck arrived in St. Louis, after purchasing the Browns in 1951, the team was nothing less than abysmal. In spite of recording their 36th win of the season during an impressive 20-to-9 thumping of the visiting Detroit Tigers, the previous afternoon, the Browns had nonetheless lost an astounding 77 games, and Veeck was desperate to boost fan attendance.

As he began to formulate his plan, he contacted a booking agent to find exactly the right individual. It wasn't as easy a task as one might think and Veeck was continually dissatisfied with the men presented to him. He was adamant that he wanted a "midget" and not a "dwarf."

A dwarf is a person with a genetic disorder and their limbs are shorter in relation to their body than normal. A midget, however, is simply a very small person who is properly formed. Veeck wanted someone who would actually look athletic in a baseball uniform.

Veeck finally assigned the job to his publicity man, Bob Fishel who ended up visiting a little guy named Eddie Gaedel who lived in Chicago. Gaedel was chosen for the job and Bill Durney, the team's traveling secretary, was assigned to pick up Gaedel and deliver him to the ballpark on the day of the double-header between the Detroit Tigers and the St. Louis Browns.

Gaedel was hidden in blankets and smuggled into the Chase Park Plaza Hotel

The 17-Inch Baseball Bat

where he was "prepped" by Veeck. He was outfitted in a uniform belonging to the nine-year-old son of Bill DeWitt, Sr. The number 6 was removed from the back of the jersey and the number "1/8" was sewn on instead The number "1/8" was also published in the official scorecard for the game and it has become a valuable collector's item.

Veeck warned Gaedel that he was not, under any circumstances, to swing at any pitches. He was told that a sniper in the stands would shoot him if he did so.

Gaedel was given a contract for $15,400, which figures out to $100 for the day, the minimum wage scale for a midget act. Gaedel waived the normal thirty-day clause that guaranteed severance pay after being released. Veeck also took out a $1,000,000 life insurance policy on Gaedel for the day in case something went cockeyed; perhaps something such as an angry pitcher clobbering a midget in the head with a 90-mile-per-hour bean-ball. Accidents do happen.

After the first game of the Browns and Tigers double-header, which the Browns lost, 5-to-2, Veeck's 50th birthday party for the American League began.

The festivities began with a parade of old automobiles driving onto the playing field. They

The 17-Inch Baseball Bat

circled near the stands so fans could get a good look at them throughout the "circus" that Veeck had prepared for them. Included were old cars that haven't been manufactured for decades; Auburn, Cord, Chalmers, Checker, Continental, Crosley, Essex, Franklin, Hudson, Kaiser, LaSalle, Lincoln, Maxwell, Nash, Oldsmobile, Packard, Pierce-Arrow, REO, Stanley-Steamer, Studebaker, Stutz, Willys, and more.

There were couples dressed in "Gay Nineties" costumes strolling through the crowd in the ballpark performing old-time songs and a two more guys, also in costume, riding around the park on old time bicycles.

A band made up of four St. Louis Browns players stood at a microphone at home plate, playing songs for the crowd.

Just like a 3-ring circus, an act was performing on each base; a hand balancing act at first base, a trampoline act on second base, and a team of jugglers on third base.

Max Patkin, the Baseball Clown, started out on the pitching mound, dancing a crazy jitterbug with a woman from the audience and then he did his "pitching wind up" schtick. He moved to home plate and with his long rubbery arms and even longer rubbery legs he went his "batting warmup" routine, got into an argument with the umpire, and followed it with a batting routine where the pitcher lobbed him a soft ball, which he dribbled off the bat, and he started to run toward third base, followed with another ar-

The 17-Inch Baseball Bat

gument when he was called out.

For the finalé, a 7-foot papier maché birthday cake was wheeled into the infield and over the public address system, Bernie Ebert's voice was heard saying, "Ladies and gentlemen—as a special present to our manager—Zack Taylor—the management is presenting him with a brand new Brownie."

Out of the cake popped the "newest" Brownie; 3-foot 7-inch Eddie Gaedel in a Browns uniform and wearing curly toed elf shoes. He waved to the appreciative crowd as he trotted off the field. When he entered the dugout, manager Zack Taylor removed Eddie's elf shoes and laced up regular cleated shoes for him.

The crowd cheered even though they had seen most of this in previous Browns games. What they couldn't be expecting was the upcoming "pièce-de-résistance" Veeck had planned. It was going to be a Doozie.

The 17-Inch Baseball Bat

Falstaff Beer Bottle Salt-and-Pepper Shakers. Miniatures given out on August 19, 1951.

The 17-Inch Baseball Bat

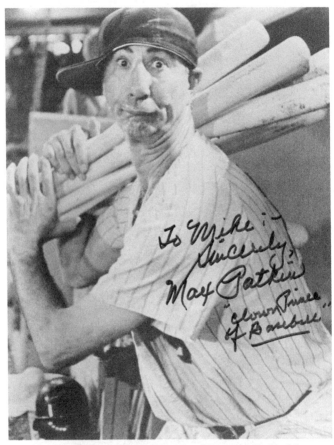

Max Patkin; Clown Prince of Baseball. Rubber faced, rubber armed, and rubber legged. His act was picked right out of a cornfield, but baseball fans loved him.

The 17-Inch Baseball Bat

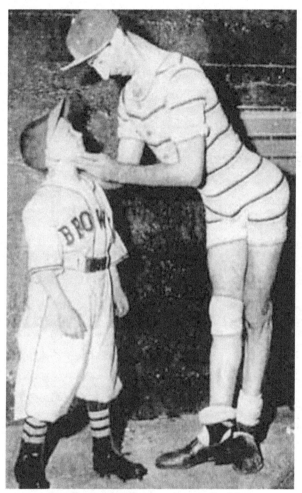

Eddie Gaedel being inspected by
Baseball Clown Max Patkin

The 17-Inch Baseball Bat

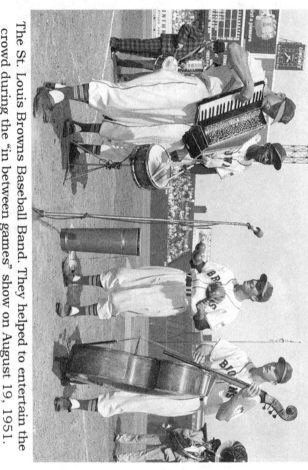

The St. Louis Browns Baseball Band. They helped to entertain the crowd during the "in between games" show on August 19, 1951.

The 17-Inch Baseball Bat

Meanwhile, in the Browns' clubhouse, Veeck's exceedingly nervous public relations man, Bob Fishel, was pacing rapidly. He was one of a handful of people who knew what was about to happen and his anxiety worsened with each step he took.

"Other then Don Larson's perfect game in 1956, when I worked for the New York Yankees, it was the most nervous I've ever been at a ballpark," Fishel told Newsday writer Joe Gergen in a 1988 interview, the same year Fishel died.

There was plenty to be nervous about, too. What would happen if Gaedel became over-excited and started swinging at every pitch? What about Bob Cain, the Tiger pitcher? What if he became angry and decided to bean-ball little Eddie with a mean fastball? What if the umpire, Ed Hurley, refused to let Gaedel bat?

A half-dozen worried men were in the room when the Browns turn came to bat in their half of the first inning of the second game.

The ballpark's Public Address speakers squawked and the announcer, Bernie Ebert, spoke slowly and distinctly. He took his time, paused his announcement in intervals with perfect timing, and proclaimed, "Ladies and gentleman . . . your attention, please . . . Coming up to bat . . . for the Browns . . . batting for Frank Saucier . . . Number . . . One-Eighth . . . Eddie . . . Gaedel!"

Not even the St. Louis Browns players had known what was going on and heads swiveled,

The 17-Inch Baseball Bat

snapping right and left when Saucier was called back to the dugout by Manager Zack Taylor.

Suddenly, astonishingly, Eddie Gaedel appeared, carrying his 17-inch, 23-ounce, "Sisler Hummel" bat, which had, appropriately enough, been manufactured in St. Louis, Missouri by the Sisler-Hummel Sporting Goods Company.

Several players shook their heads and mumbled, "What the hell?"

When Eddie reached the top of the dugout and stepped out, heading toward home plate, there was—for once—instant, absolute, and stunned silence throughout the ballpark. Frozen in time, for a few seconds, the air within Sportsman's Park ceased to exist in the vacuum of confusion and disbelief.

On that day, Jay Edson was Fishel's $65-per-week publicity assistant. Years later, he said his most vivid memory of that day came next.

For a second or two, there was literally dead silence. Everyone was dazed by the vision before them.

The single sound that could be heard was from Bill Veeck. His laughter, emanating from the Press Box, bordered on the edge of evil in its isolation. Bill had the sort of laugh that could be heard a block away and when Eddie walked onto the field, with that little bat of his, you could hear Veeck from anywhere in the ballpark.

As expected, plate umpire Hurley was immediately angered by the almost condescending and strutting approach of little Eddie Gaedel.

The 17-Inch Baseball Bat

Jim Delsing, the pinch-runner for Gaedel, remembered Hurley yelling something like, "Hey! Where the hell do you think you're going?"

"Zack Taylor knew there'd be a problem with Hurley, so he exited the dugout as Hurley began to question Eddie's appearance. Zack pulled Gaedel's signed American League contract out of his back pocket and handed it to Hurley, who took his time in reading it."

"By now, the Detroit manager, Red Rolfe, is out there with Hurley, wanting to know what's going on. And the Detroit pitcher, Bob Cain, and his catcher, Bob Swift, are talking it over, too."

Without comment, according to baseball historian, Gerald Eskenazi, Hurley handed the contract back to Zack, he gave Cain and Rolfe a long, hard look, and he simply said, 'Play ball!' "

Swift told Cain, "Keep it low." He laughed and walked back behind the plate and sat down on the ground behind home plate. Hurley ordered him into a conventional catcher's crouch, thought better of it, and allowed him to kneel on both knees.

Eddie, the ham that he was, played it for all he was worth. He kicked around some dirt in the batter's box, dug his feet in, held the bat high, and he did the best impression of Joe DiMaggio that he could muster, ready to swat a home run.

Veeck was up in the Press Box worrying, thinking, "If he swings, I'll kill him. I will kill him."

The 17-Inch Baseball Bat

Cain went into his windup, sizzled a fast-ball toward the plate, and didn't even come close to Eddie's strike zone. It didn't help that he was laughing like crazy.

"Ball one," yelled Hurley.

Cain calmed down a bit, wound up again, let fly, and it was another high fast-ball.

"Ball two," yelled Hurley.

By this time, Cain knew he was done for. He shook his head and made a motion to Swift who moved to his right, behind Gaedel, to a position for an intentional walk.

Cain lobbed the third pitch outside and high.

"Ball three," yelled Hurley.

Laughing at the absurd situation before him, Cain lobbed another one outside and high.

"Ball four!" yelled Hurley.

Later on, Cain would admit during an interview that he was scared of hitting Gaedel with a fast-ball. He knew the little guy wouldn't be able to take punishment like that and that's why he stopped trying to really pitch to him.

Cain also remembered that his one-time teammate, Dizzy Dean, told him. "If'n that there little feller wuz up there, battin' agin' me, I'd-a plunked him right between his itty-bitty eyes."

Hurley said, "Take your base," and the crowd howled as "the Littlest Brownie" trotted down to first base. He stopped twice on his journey, each time doffing his cap to the crowd along with a big wave of his little hands. Veeck was laughing the loudest of all.

The 17-Inch Baseball Bat

Eddie tagged first base, then while he waited for his pinch-runner, he held first base with one foot like the old pro he was. Taylor sent Jim Delsing in to pinch-run for him and the little guy stepped off first base with a flourish. He patted Delsing on the rump a couple of times, shook hands with the first base coach, and the fans began cheering again.

The crowd gave little Eddie a standing ovation, applauding, whistling, hooting, and laughing all the while. As he walked across the field toward the dugout, they cheered him with every step.

Eddie was, in fact, an exceptional performer in the best tradition of show business. He crossed the field one slow step at a time, stopping in between to wave his cap or to bow to the crowd.

Approaching the dugout, Eddie made a final stop. Ever the showman, he turned to the crowd, waved, bowed, tipped his St. Louis Browns cap one final time, and stepped into the dugout. He was the happiest little man you'd ever want to see. He shook hands with all the players and wore a grin from ear to ear.

He headed for the showers, and that was it. Eddie's major league baseball career was concluded.

After dressing, Eddie headed to the Press Box where he met with the St. Louis Post-Dispatch sportswriter Bob Broeg (along with others) and he gave a very short interview.

The 17-Inch Baseball Bat

Broeg later admitted he was the only sportswriter to be aware of the secret pinch-hitting event. Bob lifted Eddie up and sat him on the edge of a table for the interview.

Years later, Broeg said, "The thing I remember most vividly after all these years is how beautifully dressed the little guy was. He had on a perfectly tailored brown suit and a yellow shirt, open at the collar. He wore penny loafers but instead of pennies, he had dimes in the shoe's coin slots. He said it was more appropriate and he enjoyed the extra touch of class each "ten-cent-piece" afforded the ensemble. Anyhow, I said to him, 'Do you realize that you are now what every one of us sportswriters wishes we were? You are an ex-Big Leaguer.' "

"I guess the whole experience hadn't really hit him yet because he furrowed his brow, tilted his head, and thought for a few seconds. Then, he nodded his head, straightened up, and puffed out his chest. Without another word, he hopped down from the table, walked out, and left town, headed for Chicago. I never saw him again."

On the negative side of the event, Gaedel's appearance was less than humorous to the President of the American League, Will Harridge. He reprimanded Veeck for the stunt and Veeck responded with a letter suggesting that if little people were to be barred from baseball, he demanded that Yankee shortstop, 5-feet 6-inch Phil Rizzuto, should be immediately suspended.

Harridge did his best to make Eddie disap-

The 17-Inch Baseball Bat

pear from the record books, but ultimately his attempts failed. He ordered his statisticians to exclude Eddie's name from the 1951 records and Gaedel did not appear in the 1952 Baseball Guide.

Veeck went further and pointed out to the President of the League that if Eddie hadn't batted, then Bobby Cain hadn't thrown those pitches, and Swift hadn't caught them, and Delsing had come in to run for no one, and Saucier had been deprived of a time at bat. It would mean the continuity of baseball records were no longer intact, and the integrity of those records had been compromised.

"If Desecration of the game was the hand they wanted to play, I had a pretty strong hand myself," said Veeck.

In spite of Harridge's erroneous edicts, Eddie Gaedel's memory lives on, as well as it should. As the years slide away into the dim gossamer past, Eddie's half-inch of record space remains in the Baseball Encyclopedia. As the record reads, he's a right-handed batter and a left-handed thrower.

His listing affirms him as being 3-feet 7-inches tall, weighing 65 pounds, and he's shown to be have been a legitimate member of the St. Louis Browns baseball team. Following that is a long string of zeroes and the single numeral "1" for his walk to first base.

In the weeks following his single "at bat" appearance and the publication of the famous pic-

The 17-Inch Baseball Bat

ture of him ready to apply a vicious swat to the old spheroid tossed by Bob Cain—taken by St. Louis Post-Dispatch photographer Jack January—it was belatedly realized by Fishel that he had forgotten something extremely important.

Fishel had been so worried about everything else, he had forgotten to tell the other newspaper photographers to hang around for the first inning of the second game.

Sadly, due to Fishel's error, there are only a few photos of Eddie during his time on the field at Sportsman's Park.

On the other hand, the lack of a plethora of photos might well assist in continuing the compelling mystique surrounding the memories of the event.

Eddie attempted to shop himself around to other baseball owners and he talked quite boldly about the possibility of him confronting Bob Feller or Dizzy Trout.

On August 21, 1951, a short article appeared in the St. Louis Post-Dispatch reporting the arbitrary ban on midgets imposed by Harridge, American League president.

In response to Harridge's unilateral action, Eddie was quoted, "Naturally, I feel kinda down—but, at least, I've got the memory of playing as a major leaguer for 30 seconds and that's something nobody can take away from me. I really didn't expect to get as far as home plate and be able to bat. I didn't think the umpire would let me bat no matter what sort of contract

The 17-Inch Baseball Bat

I had. But when he did, then I thought that everything was okay and the contract would stand up. I expected to go up to bat in about 10 games for the Browns. I was set to get $100 every time I made an appearance at the plate for the Browns. I've got a clipping of the box score and my name is there in black and white. What other midget can say the same?"

Believe it or not, another 8-innings of baseball was still left to play following the "midget episode."

If the Gods had been smiling at the Browns that day, Delsing, running for Gaedel, would have scored and the Browns would have won the game 1-0, but the Gods, as we all know, are fickle and petulant.

Veeck later said, "I was willing to win by a single run, regardless of the final score, as long as that run represented Eddie Gaedel."

But was not to be. Delsing reached as far as third base with only one out but he was left stranded. The Browns lost the second game, 6-2.

The 17-Inch Baseball Bat

While the Detroit Tigers were batting during the top half of the first inning, Eddie was getting ready. Eddie had removed his "elf shoes" and Zack Taylor is lacing up his cleats in preparation for Eddie's turn at bat.

Eddie's all ready to go. He's moving around in the dugout, meeting the rest of the team.

The 17-Inch Baseball Bat

Everyone's watching a pop fly for the third out of the Tigers in the first inning. It's almost time for Eddie to make his debut.

The 17-Inch Baseball Bat

The bottom of the first inning is starting and Eddie is getting last minute instructions from Zack Taylor.

The 17-Inch Baseball Bat

After Eddie nonchalantly meanders to the on deck area, Umpire Hurley calls Zack Taylor out of the dugout to ask what's going on. Luckily, Zack had the signed, legal contract in his back pocket ready for Hurley's challenge.

The 17-Inch Baseball Bat

Like the old pro he is, Eddie ignores the legal
shanagians going on behind him as he
continues to limber up with swinging
and stretching exercises.

The 17-Inch Baseball Bat

The situation has been discussed, Zack has shown
a legal, signed contract with Eddie's name on it,
and Umpire Hurley has just given the
green light to "Play Ball!"

The 17-Inch Baseball Bat

Two slightly different viewpoints of Eddie in the Batter's Box. Only two more balls to go for a walk.

The 17-Inch Baseball Bat

Eddie Gaedel pinch-hitting for Frank Saucier.
August 19, 1951.

The 17-Inch Baseball Bat

Eddie has just been relieved at first base by pinch-runner Jim Delsing. Eddie took his time, making a complete performance of walking across the field, waving, bowing, and tipping his cap to the crowd. He was a showman all the way!

The 17-Inch Baseball Bat

Eddie gives one final tip of the Brownie cap
before leaving the field and heading into
the dugout. It's been one hell of a day!

The 17-Inch Baseball Bat

Eddie Gaedel.
The Littlest Brownie!

The 17-Inch Baseball Bat

The 17-Inch Baseball Bat

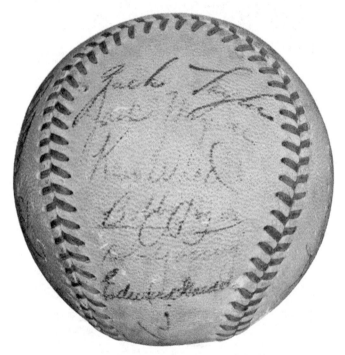

A game ball from the Tigers and Browns
double-header on August 19, 1951
with Eddie's signature.

The 17-Inch Baseball Bat

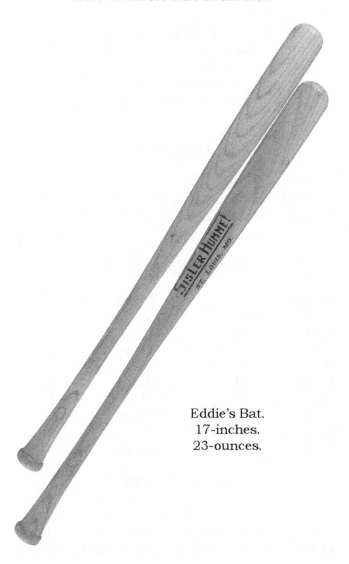

Eddie's Bat.
17-inches.
23-ounces.

The 17-Inch Baseball Bat

GAME TWO
Sunday, August 19, 1951
Sportsman's Park III
2-Hours, 24 Minutes
Attendance: 18369

UMPIRES

HP: Eddie Hurley.
1B: Art Passarella (left in the 4th inning).
3B; Joe Paparella (Move to 1B in 4th inning).

STARTING LINEUP

Tigers		**Browns**	
Priddy	2b	Saucier	rf
Kryhoski	1b	Young	2b
Kell	3b	Mapes	cf
Wertz	rf	Lollar	c
Mullin	cf	Wood	lf
Souchock	lf	Arft	1b
Swift	c	Marsh	3b
Berry	ss	Jennings	ss
Cain	p	Pillette	p

FIRST INNING

Tigers
Priddy out on an unknown play; Kryhoski walked; Lollar allowed a passed ball and Kry-

The 17-Inch Baseball Bat

hoski moved to second; Kell walked; Wertz out on an unknown play; Mullin out on an unknown play.

0-Runs; 0-Hits; 0-Errors, 2-Left on base.
Tigers 0, Browns 0.

Browns

Gaedel batted for Saucier; Gaedel walked; Delsing ran for Gaedel; Young out on an unknown play; Mapes singled and Delsing moved to second; Lollar out on an unknown play; Wood walked and Delsing moved to third, Mapes moved to second; Arft out on an unknown play.

0-Runs; 1-Hit; 0-Errors; 3 Left on base.
Tigers 0, Browns 0.

SECOND INNING

Tigers

Delsing stayed in game, playing CF; Mapes changed positions, playing RF; Souchock out on an unknown play; Swift struck out; Berry out on an unknown play.

0-Runs; 0-Hits; 0-Errors; 0-Left on base.
Tigers 0, Browns 0.

Browns

Marsh doubled; Jennings out on an unknown play; Pillette out on an unknown play; Delsing

The 17-Inch Baseball Bat

struck out.

0-Runs; 1-Hit; 0-Errors; 1-Left on base.
Tigers 0, Browns 0.

THIRD INNING

Tigers

Cain struck out; Priddy out on an unknown play; Kryhoski out on an unknown play.

0-Runs; 0-Hits; 0-Errors; 0-Left on base.
Tigers 0, Browns 0.

Browns

Young singled; Mapes singled, Young moved to second; Lollar grounded into a double-play (third to first), and Mapes moved to second, Young out at third; Wood out on an unknown play.

0-Runs; 2-Hits; 0-Errors; 1-Left on base.
Tigers 0, Browns 0.

FOURTH INNING

Tigers

Kell out on an unknown play; Wertz out on an unknown play; Mullin doubled; Souchock singled and Mullin scored; Souchock was caught stealing second; 1B umpire injured ankle when he stepped on a ball while teams

The 17-Inch Baseball Bat

were changing sides; 3B umpire Paparella moved to 1st and the game was finished with 3 umpires.

1-Run; 2-Hits; 0-Errors; 0-Left on base.
Tigers 1, Browns 0.

Browns

Arft out on an unknown play; Marsh out on an unknown play; Jennings out on an unknown play.

0-Runs; 0-Hits; 0-Errors; 0-Left on base.
Tigers 1, Browns 0.

FIFTH INNING

Tigers

Swift out on an unknown play; Berry out on an unknown play; Cain out on an unknown play.

0-Runs; 0-Hits; 0-Errors; 0-Left on base.
Tigers 1, Browns 0.

Browns

Keller replaced Wertz, playing RF; Pillette out on an unknown play; Delsing walked; Young out on an unknown play; Mapes out on an unknown play.

0-Runs; 0-Hits; 0-Errors; 1-Left on base.
Tigers 1, Browns 0.

The 17-Inch Baseball Bat

SIXTH INNING

Tigers

Priddy homered; Kryhoski struck out; Kell singled; Keller out on an unknown play; Mullin doubled, moving Kell to third; Souchock walked; Swift out on an unknown play.

1-Run; 3-Hits; 0-Errors; 3 Left on base.
Tigers 2, Browns 0.

Browns

Lollar reached on an error by Kell and Lollar made second base; Wood doubled and Lollar scored (unearned); Arft reached on a fielder's choice and Wood was out at third; Marsh reached on an error by Kell and Arft was out at third while Marsh moved to second; Jennings reached on an error by Berry and Marsh scored (unearned–no RBI); Pillette walked, moving Jennings to second; Delsing out on an unknown play.

2-Runs; 1-Hit; 3-Errors; 2 Left on base.
Tigers 2, Browns 2.

SEVENTH INNING

Tigers

Berry out on an unknown play; Cain walked; Priddy out on an unknown play; Kryhoski singled, moving Cain to second; Kell singled,

The 17-Inch Baseball Bat

moving Cain to third and Kryhoski to second; Keller singled, Cain scored and Kryhoski scored, Kell moved to third; Mullin singled, moving Keller to second; Suchecki replaced Pillette (pitching); Souchock out on an unknown play.

    3-Runs; 4-Hits; 0-Errors, 2-Left on base.
            Tigers 5, Browns 2.

Browns

Young out on an unknown play; Mapes out on an unknown play; Lollar out on an unknown play.

    0-Runs; 0-Hits; 0-Errors; 0-Left on base.
            Tigers 5, Browns 2.

EIGHTH INNING

Tigers

Swift singled; Lipon ran for Swift; Berry out on an unknown play; Cain out on a sacrifice bunt, moving Lipon to second; Priddy reached on an error by Young. Lipon scored (unearned–no RBI); Kryhoski out on an unknown play.

    1-Run; 1-Hit; 1-Error; 1-Left on base.
            Tigers 6, Browns 2.

Browns

Ginsberg replaced Lipon, playing C; Wood singled; Arft out on an unknown play; Marsh

The 17-Inch Baseball Bat

out on an unknown play; Jennings out on an unknown play.

0-Runs; 1-Hit; 0-Errors; 1-Left on base.
Tigers 6, Browns 2.

NINTH INNING

Tigers

Kell singled; Keller out on a sacrifice bunt; Kell moved to second; Mullin out on an unknown play; Souchock out on an unknown play.

0-Runs; 1-Hit; 0-Errors; 1-Left on base.
Tigers 6, Browns 2.

Browns

Maguire batted for Suchecki; Maguire out on an unknown play; Delsing doubled; Young walked; Trout replaced Cain (pitching); Mapes out on an unknown play; Lollar struck out.

0-Runs; 1-Hit; 0-Errors; 2-Left on base.
Tigers 6, Browns 2.

Final Totals	R	H	E	LOB
Tigers	6	11	3	9
Browns	2	7	1	11

The 17-Inch Baseball Bat

Detroit Tigers 6 55-60	Sunday, August 19, 1951 Attendance: 18,369 Venue: Sportsman's Park Game Duration: 2:24 Day Game, on grass									St. Louis Browns 2 36-79		
		1	2	3	4	5	6	7	8	9	R	H	E
Detroit Tigers		0	0	0	1	0	1	3	1	0	6	11	3
St. Louis Browns		0	0	0	0	0	2	0	0	0	2	7	1
WP: Bob Cain (10-9) • LP: Duane Pillette (5-13) • SV: Dizzy Trout (6)													

[59]

The 17-Inch Baseball Bat

St. Louis Browns

Batting	AB	R	H	RBI	BB	SO	PA	BA	OBP	SLG	OPS	PO	A	Details
Frank Saucier RF	0	0	0	0	0	0	0		.333			0	0	
Eddie Gaedel PH	0	0	0	0	1	0	1		1.000					
Jim Delsing PR-CF	3	0	0	0	1	0	4	.111	.222	.222	.556	3	0	2B
Bobby Young 2B	4	0	1	0	1	1	5	.270	.366	.396	.762	2	2	
Cliff Mapes CF-RF	5	0	1	0	0	0	5	.268	.315	.328	.642	2	0	
Sherm Lollar C	5	0	2	0	0	0	5	.232	.304	.392	.696	1	0	
Ken Wood LF	5	1	0	0	0	1	5	.258	.374	.411	.785	4	1	GDP
Hank Arft 1B	3	0	2	1	1	0	4	.202	.265	.381	.645	4	0	2B
Fred Marsh 3B	4	0	0	0	0	0	4	.276	.360	.420	.780	9	0	
Bill Jennings SS	4	1	1	0	0	0	4	.214	.272	.297	.569	1	3	2B
Duane Pillette P	4	0	0	0	0	0	4	.165	.204	.252	.456	3	4	
Jim Suchecki P	2	0	0	0	1	0	3	.089	.196	.089	.285	0	0	
Jack Maguire PH	0	0	0	0	0	0	0	.143	.200	.143	.343	0	0	
	1	0	0	0	0	0	1	.271	.322	.368	.690			
Team Totals	35	2	7	1	5	2	40	.200	.300	.286	.586	27	10	

The 17-Inch Baseball Bat

Detroit Tigers

Batting	AB	R	H	RBI	BB	SO	PA	BA	OBP	SLG	OPS	PO	A	Details
Jerry Priddy 2B	5	1	1	1	0	0	5	.265	.340	.367	.707	2	2	HR
Dick Kryhoski 1B	4	1	1	0	1	1	5	.292	.333	.433	.766	7	1	
George Kell 3B	4	1	3	0	1	0	5	.339	.409	.407	.815	3	3	
Vic Wertz RF	2	0	0	0	0	0	2	.283	.388	.492	.880	1	0	
Charlie Keller RF	2	0	1	2	0	0	3	.259	.385	.407	.792	2	0	SH
Pat Mullin CF	5	1	3	1	0	0	5	.298	.385	.531	.915	2	0	2:2B
Bud Souchock LF	4	0	1	1	1	0	5	.254	.336	.546	.882	4	0	CS
Bob Swift C	4	0	1	0	0	1	4	.220	.264	.220	.484	2	0	
Johnny Lipon PR	0	1	0	0	0	0	0	.265	.331	.296	.627			
Joe Ginsberg C	0	0	0	0	0	0	0	.259	.353	.396	.749	1	0	
Neil Berry SS	4	0	0	0	0	0	4	.233	.276	.275	.551	2	1	
Bob Cain P	2	1	0	0	1	1	4	.217	.294	.304	.598	1	1	SH
Dizzy Trout P	0	0	0	0	0	0	0	.261	.382	.348	.730	0	0	
Team Totals	36	6	11	5	4	3	42	.306	.375	.444	.819	27	8	

The 17-Inch Baseball Bat

Chapter Four

The Cast Of Characters

Bill Veeck

If it weren't for his father—William Louis Veeck, Sr.—it could well be that Bill, Jr. might have found a career in a profession other than baseball. The story is that Bill Jr.'s father was a sportswriter for the old Chicago American newspaper and he was more often than not, highly critical of the management of William Wrigley's Chicago Cubs baseball team. At that time, Bill, Sr. used the newspaperman "nom de plume" of Bill Bailey.

Finally tiring of reading the dismal reportage of his team, Mr. Wrigley contacted Bill, Sr. and told him, "If you think you know so much, I dare you to take over the team and prove you know more and can do better," to which Bill, Sr. quickly replied, "I'd be glad to."

This happened in 1918, when Bill, Jr. was a mere four years old, having been born in Chicago on February 9, 1914. By the time Bill, Jr. was ten years old, he was thoroughly enamored of the "school of the spheroid" and his father let

The 17-Inch Baseball Bat

him work as a vendor, ticket seller, grounds-keeper, general Go-Fer, and any other odd jobs the young lad could do to keep busy and earn a few dollars.

Bill, Sr. proved to be worth his salt in the world of professional baseball and he provided Mr. Wrigley with a highly competitive team that won pennants in 1929 and 1932. Sadly, Bill, Sr. died in 1933 from leukemia.

With his father's death, Bill, Jr. had to drop out of Kenyon College to earn a living. He had always been a rowdy, disruptive, party-happy student anyway, so it wasn't a difficult choice.

In spite of the father and son being complete opposites, Bill, Jr. loved and respected his father greatly. Bill, Sr. was of the old school, a formal gentleman who was the picture-perfect vision of establishment dignity. Bill, Jr., conversely, was a bit wild, hated ties, wore gaudy sport-shirts, and tilted at any windmill available while he bucked the system on the slightest whim.

Upon his father's death, Bill talked himself into a full-time, paying job with the Cubs and he continued to study and learn both the game and the business side of the game. In 1935, with a salary of $18 a week, he married Eleanor Raymond who had been an elephant "wrangler" and bareback rider with the Ringling Brothers, and Barnum & Bailey Circus.

Proving his ability as a fast-talking promoter and wheeler-dealer, Bill bought his first ball-club when he was 27 years old, taking possession of

The 17-Inch Baseball Bat

the Milwaukee Brewers in 1941, It was a match made in heaven and since the Brewers were basement dwellers, there was no further descent available to the team. Using the newly purchased Brewers as a testing tool, Bill began to audition his baseball philosophy, his marketing skills, and his promotional schemes. He painted the dilapidated old park, he gave away prizes almost every night. He scheduled morning games for overnight workers and he served them cornflake breakfasts. He began to make a name for himself as someone who believed baseball should be, first and foremost, fun for everyone.

Equally important, he proved that he knew the game of baseball and how to operate a team. He bought good players on borrowed money, sold them at a profit, and used the profits to buy more good players. In his first year as an owner, he built a highly competitive team and nearly won the old American Association's pennant in 1942, his first full season. Even better, he won the next three pennants in a row.

Then World War II got in the way. Along with many other service qualified baseball people, Veeck joined the Marines in 1943, was stationed in the South Pacific island of Bougainville, and he suffered a terribly debilitating injury when an anti-aircraft gun almost destroyed his right foot. The gun had somehow recoiled improperly and dug a huge gash in his foot. The injury became infected and Bill spent the rest of the war in naval hospitals while the foot was op-

The 17-Inch Baseball Bat

erated on numerous times. His foot eventually had to be amputated. In spite of everything—and from his hospital bed—he continued to run the Brewers through a long-distance letter writing campaign.

Bill was finally mustered out in 1945 and by that time, his marriage was in trouble. He ended up having to sell the Brewers to pay the divorce settlement.

On a positive note, with his marriage ended, Bill had time on his hands so he put together a syndicate and he bought another bottom dwelling team, the Cleveland Indians. He was, once again, giving away nightly prizes, exploding fireworks at every game, pulling crazy stunts, and doing anything else he hoped would get the paying public into a ballpark seat.

He also discovered, to his regret, that the "big-league" owners were not as accepting of his stunts, tricks, giveaways, and promotions as the minor-league owners were, but Bill never let a minor detail like that bother him.

The general consensus of the big-league owners was that Veeck and his cavalier folderol should not be allowed to befoul the stately and noble environs of a Major League Baseball Park—heaven forbid. George Weiss, the Yankees' general manager once struck down the idea of giving away Yankee baseball caps at a game with the comment, "I don't want every kid in New York walking around in a Yankee cap!"

In response to sneers toward his "low brow"

The 17-Inch Baseball Bat

promotional philosophy, Bill once said, "My tastes, I have discovered, are so average and so common, that any sort of entertaining idea I might enjoy would most probably appeal to most, if not all, of our teams' customers. As far as I'm concerned, every day at the ballpark is Mardi Gras and every fan walking through the turnstile is king or queen for the day." Bill's philosophy was quite apparently close to the hearts and minds of Cleveland Indians fans. In 1946, he had pushed the previously lagging attendance to over one million ticket buyers. He knew what he was doing.

Unfortunately, he did not know what he was doing when he tried to reconcile with his wife during the 1946 World Series. He paid more attention to his clientele and his guests than to Eleanor and she walked out—again—before the series was finished, never to return. His marriage was completely, irrevocably over.

Also during that series, Bill's leg had been bothering him more than usual and he discovered that the infection causing the amputation of his foot had spread through the bone tissue of his leg and it had to be amputated up to the knee. As always, Bill tried to put a positive spin on the situation and when his new artificial leg arrived, he threw a party to celebrate. Little by little, over the years, problems with his leg continued to plague him and he lost more and more of the limb as the infection continued to spread up from the stump. He endured a total of

The 17-Inch Baseball Bat

36 operations on the leg and still lost most of it.

In spite of everything, Bill focused on the job at hand, building a winning baseball team, and in 1948, his Cleveland Indians won the Pennant and they continued their dominance to beat the Boston Braves in six games. That victory could, arguably, be considered the highlight of Bill's life. From then on, nothing he did matched his accomplishments in Cleveland.

With his marriage in tatters, he complained that, "I had never been more lonely in my life."

The next year, the Indians ended up in third place, Bill rarely saw his three children, and he never saw his ex-wife. Ellen, too, became withdrawn and the entire family seemed to fall apart.

Bill decided to change everything, even to the point of selling the Cleveland Indians. It was then that Bill met Mary Frances Ackerman, a publicist for the Ice Capades. They were married on April 29, 1950, and it turned out to be a perfect match. She became as involved with baseball as Bill was, she shared the limelight with him on radio and television shows, and in between all of that, the couple had six children.

Champing at the bit to get back into "the game" Bill purchased the St. Louis Browns in July, 1951. The Browns gave new meaning to the term "bottom dweller" and if Bill thought he would be able to do the same thing with them as he did with the Indians, he was quickly disabused of the idea. He was quoted in the Post-

The 17-Inch Baseball Bat

Dispatch newspaper as claiming that he would soon be, "running the Cardinals out of town."

After reading that, one of the Post-Dispatch subscribers wrote a "letter to the editor" asking when Bill was going to his tailor to be fitted for a straight-jacket.

In spite of everything he did, he failed to make headway with the hapless Browns. Even the outlandish "Eddie Gaedel Affair" couldn't save the Browns and although the fans loved it, Bill had created even more determined enemies of the other owners in the American League.

Although Bill attempted to make a deal to move the Browns to Baltimore, the rest of the league owners had to approve the move and they all voted against it. Bill always claimed the owners were simply "malicious" in their opposition to his plans.

It wasn't merely the stunts, promotions, and the rest of the "Veeck Baggage" that bothered the other owners so much. Bill had angered all of the owners by demanding that visiting teams share in the television revenues of the hosting team. This, said the owners, was simply a socialistic scheme and absolutely un-American.

During his tenure with the Browns, Bill was continually selling off his good players to pay for the rest of the team. Even his ballpark proved to be a problem for him. He had to pay for the upkeep, insurance, and all the other "overhead" to keep the park up and running. His opponents, the Cardinals, just rented the place,

The 17-Inch Baseball Bat

played there, and then went home.

Running out of money, Bill ended up selling Sportsman's Park to Augie Busch, Jr., the owner of Anheuser-Busch brewery and the Cardinals baseball team, for $800,000 in cash. In 1953 he sold off more of his best players as well as his Arizona ranch, just to tread water.

In their last game in 1953, the Browns ran out of new baseballs and had to use old, scuffed, warm-up balls. After another vote to move his team to Baltimore was, once again, vetoed by the other owners, Bill was at the end of his rope; actually, he didn't even own enough rope to hang himself.

Bill accepted the inevitable and sold his Brownies to a Baltimore syndicate that had made an offer for the team. Instantly, a vote was held and the league approved the transfer and a name change to the "Orioles."

The rest of the league owners didn't care if they froze him out, bought him out, or bankrupted him. After five years, they had finally gotten even with him for his brashness and his disturbance of the old, established, order of things.

For the next three years, Bill kept searching for a way back, a new path back to the Valhalla of baseball. He tried to buy the Detroit Tigers, tried to get a team established on the West Coast, tried to buy the Ringling Brothers and Barnum & Baily circus saying that everyone always told him he should be in the circus anyway, he scouted for the Cleveland Indians, he

The 17-Inch Baseball Bat

ran the Triple-A Miami Marlins for a season, and he served as commentator of NBC's Game of the Week—he kept busy.

In 1958, lightning stuck. Chicago White Sox president, Grace Comiskey, died and left her baseball stock to her daughter, Dorothy Rigney instead of her son, Charles Comiskey, who bitterly resented the action. A vicious family squabble ensued and to make a long story short, Bill Veeck, along with Hank Greenberg, managed to obtain a majority of White Sox stock. Chuck Comiskey despised Bill, but Bill did his best to ignore him and get on with the business of baseball.

Bill Veeck was back and so were his promotions and stunts—big time. He began a "one thousand" campaign in which a "lucky chair" won 1,000 cans of beer, or 1,000 pies, or 1,000 bottles of root beer, or 1,000 cupcakes, or anything else that would come to him out of the blue. He staged "cab driver day," "bartender day," etc. When outfielder Al Smith was booed by fans, he began to let anyone named Al Smith in for free as the outfielder's guest. There was nothing he wouldn't do to get a fan into the ballpark and into a seat.

The first year Bill and Hank ran the team, the White Sox took possession of first place on July 28, 1959 and stayed there to clinch the pennant. It was the first White Sox series since the infamous "Black Sox" team scandal.

Bill jokingly said, "Who ever thought a team

The 17-Inch Baseball Bat

could win a pennant strictly on pitching, good defense, and speed running the bases? This is contrary to everything I ever learned about baseball," and he gave all of the credit for the pennant to manager Al Lopez.

The White Sox, however, couldn't sustain the fight. They lost the World Series to the Los Angeles Dodgers and a joke began to make the rounds that, "The White Sox will change their name to the White Nylons because nylons get more runs." Baseball has always had a full complement of comedians.

1960 was another innovative year for Bill Veeck. That year he put player's names on the backs of their road uniforms and followed it in 1961 with names on their home uniforms.

1960 was also the year Bill put up his "exploding scoreboard." In an interview, Bill said, "It shrieks, it wiggles, it burps, it whines, and it twinkles. Fireworks explode beneath the scoreboard while tape recordings blast virtually every sound imaginable; a cavalry charge, machine-gun fire, trains in a head-on crash, jet bombers, and a woman screaming, 'Fireman, save my child.' " The fans loved it and visiting teams hated it with a passion.

Bill was forced to retire in 1961 due to extreme health problems and in 1962 (with sportswriter Ed Linn) he wrote his autobiography "Veeck as in Wreck."

He sold his share of the White Sox to one of his partners, Arthur Allyn, Jr. He bought a farm

The 17-Inch Baseball Bat

in Maryland on the shores of Chesapeake Bay, named it "Tranquility," and he moved his family there.

Although he took it easy for the most part, Bill kept busy writing newspaper columns, watching Little League games, and writing two more books; "The Hustler's Handbook" and "Thirty Tons a Day."

By 1970, Bill's health had improved greatly and his old baseball itch was in need of a good scratching. He tried to buy the Washington expansion team but missed out and then he made an offer on the Baltimore Orioles but the owner backed out of the deal at the last moment.

The Chicago White Sox suddenly came up for sale in 1975 due to bankruptcy problems of Bill's friend and former partner Arthur Allyn, Jr. The team was on the verge of purchase and transfer to Seattle, Washington when 61-year-old Bill put together a syndicate of more than 40 investors, including his old buddy, Hank Greenberg.

The purchase was rejected outright by the rest of the American League team owners. The reason given was that the deal was too "dependent" on borrowed money, but the real reason was the same old contempt for Bill Veeck. He had made many enemies over the years and they had long memories.

Bill raised a large amount of cash, but he was voted down yet again. They were teaching him a lesson, pure and simple. Finally, one of

The 17-Inch Baseball Bat

the owners came to his senses and put business before hatred. Detroit Tigers owner John Fetzer told the other owners, "I don't like him any more than you gentlemen do. He's called me a son-of-a-bitch more times that I can count but this is simply a business transaction, nothing more, nothing less. We need to take another vote."

They bit their tongues, held their ire, and took the vote. Bill was approved 10-2.

Bill was back—again.

1977 was the last great year for Bill. He invented a team made up of "rented players" who were a year away from free agency, knowing he could not afford them the following year. They were called the "South Side Hit Men," they hit 192 home runs and won 90 games, but they couldn't keep it up. The White Sox slid to third place and missed the pennant. Bill broke his own attendance record with more than 1.6 million fans in the seats and he was named the Major League Executive of the Year by "The Sporting News." The other owners were probably gnashing their teeth, but such is the game.

The next year was the start of a downward spiral and Bill had no way out. He said, "We will scheme, connive, steal, and do everything possible to win a pennant—except pay huge "free agent" salaries for ballplayers.

The nadir of his second go-around with the White Sox came with the worst stunt ever devised in the history of baseball. On July 12, 1979, Bill hosted what he called "Disco Demoli-

The 17-Inch Baseball Bat

tion Night." The idea was simple; bring a disco record, pay 98-cents for admission, and watch as the collected records were blown up between games of a double-header.

Poor Bill hadn't considered the type of "fan" he was inviting into the ballpark that day. After a pile of records had been demolished in a huge explosion, there was a massive hole in the outfield and pieces of records were everywhere.

The overflow crowd crashed through and destroyed the gates, people began to "sail" records all over the ballpark, and onto the field. Beer filled their bellies and marijuana smoke filled the stands. The berserk "fans" broke onto the field and ran amuck, destroying almost everything. They even stole all of the bases.

It was impossible to continue with baseball and the second game wasn't even started, it was forfeited to the Detroit Tigers.

The next year, 1980, Bill's luck, money, and health had all run out. His incessant chain-smoking had produced emphysema, his eyesight and hearing were almost gone, and he had one final surgery on his ever-diminishing right leg.

A big-time Chicago real estate magnate, by the name of Jerry Reinsdorf, and a television entrepreneur, named Eddie Einhorn, bought the White Sox. At their first press conference, Einhorn angered Bill by saying, "We're changing things; we're going to run a high-class baseball team. We are going to turn the ballpark into a

The 17-Inch Baseball Bat

family-friendly place where everyone can enjoy a baseball game. We are not continuing with Bill Veeck's idea of running the world's largest out-door saloon."

Bill retaliated by changing his allegiance and becoming a Cubs fan. From then on, he regularly showed up at Wrigley Field and sat with the rest of the raucous crowd in the bleachers.

In 1984, a visit to the doctor discovered his lungs to be riddled with cancer and Bill Veeck died on January 2, 1986 at the age of 71.

In spite of the many obstacles confronting him throughout his life, including other baseball team owners, Bill Veeck was inducted into the Baseball Hall of Fame in 1991. Once he was dead, his enemies could no longer keep him from his due. His Cooperstown plaque reads, "A Champion of the Little Guy."

The 17-Inch Baseball Bat

Bill Veeck, Sr. gave his son, Bill, Jr. his start in professional baseball.

The 17-Inch Baseball Bat

The 17-Inch Baseball Bat

Bill Veeck

William "Bill" Veeck, Jr., was born in 1914, the son of a former president of the Chicago Cubs organization. One of the most colorful and innovative executives in the history of baseball, Bill Veeck was elected to the Ohio Baseball Hall of Fame in 1979.

Bill began his carrer as owner and operator of a highly successful franchise in Milwaukee in 1940. He purchased the Cleveland Indians and combined special promotions with a winning club to lure 2,620,627 fans to Municipal Stadium, and set an attendance record that stands to this date. Veeck also owned for a time teams in Chicago and St. Louis. At St. Louis, he sent midget Eddie Gaedel to the plate against the Tigers in one of baseball's most interesting stunts.

Some of the Veeck's contributions to baseball include placing players' names on the backs of their uniforms and scoreboards that explode when homeruns are hit. A racing buff, too, Veeck showed his love for fans by giving them his phone number and spending hours evaluating their opinions.

The 17-Inch Baseball Bat

Young Bill Veeck. He condescended to wear a jacket, but still no necktie. He hadn't started his sportshirt phase yet.

The 17-Inch Baseball Bat

Bill in his Cleveland Indians office in 1949.
In the background is the 1948 World Series
Championship Cup. It also looks like
Bill enjoyed a "chaw o' tabbacky"
every now and then.

The 17-Inch Baseball Bat

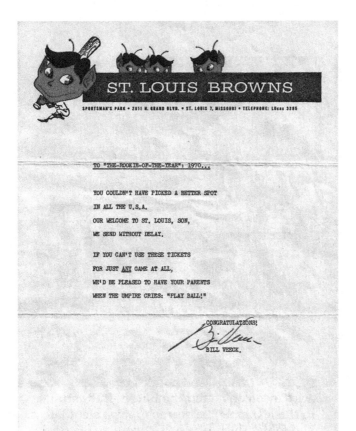

A good example of the type of letter Bill Veeck would send to people. He always thought a person should have fun at a ballbark.

The 17-Inch Baseball Bat

Zack Taylor was often the butt of Bill's stunts.
In this example, he seems to have slept late
and forgot there was a ball game today. Not
to worry, though, Bill & the gang will make
sure he gets to the dugout in time.

The 17-Inch Baseball Bat

Another imaginative stunt from the comedy duo of Veeck & Taylor! In this offering, the fans behind the dugout are allowed to "manage" the team. Zack Taylor, "unnecessary" to the game, sat next to the dugout in his rocking chair while smoking his pipe and wearing "civies." Believe it or not, the Browns won the game!

The 17-Inch Baseball Bat

The other team owners in the American League might well have disliked, even hated, Bill Veeck, but the fans loved him. He thought baseball wasn't just a business, it was first and foremost a game to be enjoyed.

The 17-Inch Baseball Bat

Disco Destruction Night! How could Bill not know that blowing up a massive pile of disco records would also blow a hole in the outfield? Live and learn, eh? Add the pot smokers and the drunks and you've got a major disaster in the making. And, there wasn't a midget in sight.

The 17-Inch Baseball Bat

Ever since the injury and infection of Bill's right
foot with the Marine's in World War II, it never
healed properly. It gave him trouble
the rest of his life.

The 17-Inch Baseball Bat

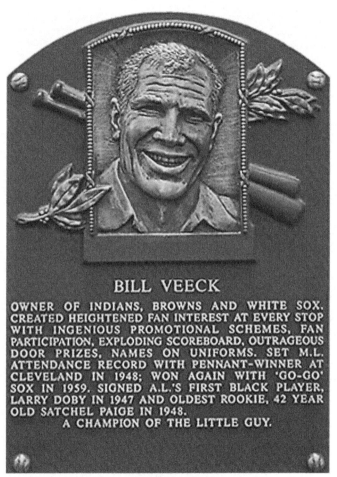

Bill Veeck's plaque in the Baseball Hall of Fame.

The 17-Inch Baseball Bat

Eddie Gaedel

Edward Carl Gaedel was born in Chicago, Illinois on June 8, 1925, the second of three children born to Carl and Helen Gaedele. Early in his life, Eddie dropped the last "e" from the family name to make the name more "marketable." Even in high school, Eddie dreamed of becoming an actor and making it big in the entertainment world. He did, in fact, make it big but his celebrity and popularity failed to endure for long.

His father, Carl, had immigrated to the United States from Lithuania in 1902 and he settled in Chicago thinking that a big city would be a good place to find work. He did find work, but it was just enough to make a paycheck-to-paycheck living for his family. He became a shoe salesman in a local department store.

Eddie's mother, Helen Janicki, was born in New York City to parents who had also immigrated to the United States. Her parents, however, came from Poland. How Helen got to Chicago is a mystery, but that's where she ended up to meet and marry Carl Gaedel in 1919.

The familiar family story is that little Eddie was born as a healthy and happy little boy and

The 17-Inch Baseball Bat

he had a normal childhood up to his third birthday. For some reason, he simply stopped growing. His parents took him to a number of doctors and he was checked from head to foot. Tests were made, and nothing could be found to explain his cessation of growth. One doctor ventured a hypothesis that it might be a "possible thyroid problem." The doctor was unable to say for certain this was the cause of Eddie's problem and neither could he do anything to rectify the condition; it would, however, be a certainty that he sent a bill to the saddened parents.

A couple of years later, Eddie's growth resumed, but it was very slow and by the time he had graduated from high school, he had reached his maximum height, a total of 43-inches tall; 3-feet and 7-inches in his stocking feet. At full growth, he weighed 65-pounds and it only altered slightly in accordance with his amount and sort of food consumption. Eddie's two siblings, as well as his parents, were of normal height and stature.

As a consequence of his stunted height, Eddie suffered greatly throughout his life, in spite of his fame and occasional fortune. The saddest part of the situation would have to be attributed to Eddie, himself, and his ingrained reaction to the life that fate had dealt him.

It was known that Eddie had been picked on throughout his school years and had been taunted as a child. A large chip grew on Eddie's shoulder and he began to not only reply to such

The 17-Inch Baseball Bat

aggravation and teasing with fisticuffs, he was often the one who started, or escalated, the trouble. Later in life, when he turned to alcohol for solace, he would often look for the slightest reason to pick a fight with a much larger person. For good or bad, it must be acknowledged that Eddie was certainly no coward when the "beer muscles" took over. He would never back down once a challenge had been made.

By the time Eddie was nearing graduation from high school, he began to consider his future. In his high school yearbook, next to his photo his name is listed as Edward Gaedel with the sobriquet of "Shorty" underneath. Also indicated is that he was a Hall Guard, a member of the Sports Club, and that his ambition was to become an Actor.

During his high school years, Eddie made extra money doing odd jobs for neighbors. He also had a part-time job as an errand boy for the local newspaper, "The Drover's Daily Journal," which started in 1873 in newspaper format, became a monthly magazine, and is still in publication as a report on the Chicago Stockyards.

Following graduation, Eddie worked in a number of jobs. It's often incorrectly reported that he was a "Munchkin" in the motion-picture "Wizard of Oz," but that would have been impossible. Eddie was born in 1925 and the movie was made in 1939, when he was 14 years old. Also, Eddie disliked traveling. When he did travel, it was only for a job and only under spe-

The 17-Inch Baseball Bat

cific circumstances. Eddie had a "comfort zone" in his neighborhood, and he was reticent to leave it for anything except an exceptional job.

One of his better paying jobs was with the Douglas Aircraft Company as a riveter and electric wirer for the DC-4 Skymaster, an upgraded version of the magnificent DC-3 aircraft. Being of small size, Eddie could get into small spaces and accomplish jobs that larger people couldn't.

Built during World War II and the Korean War the SkyMaster was manufactured in both California and Illinois. The Illinois plant built a total of 655 Skymaster aircraft at Orchard Place/Douglas Field in the unincorporated area of Cook County, near Chicago. The field later became O'Hare International Airport.

In spite of his job with Douglas, Eddie continued his dreams of being an actor, which was odd in a sense, because actors must be where the jobs are. If an actor is unwilling to travel, it drastically lowers the prospects for a real career of "treading the boards." But Eddie kept the dream alive, no matter how ill-reasoned.

Following the end of World War II, Eddie gave up the job at Douglas Aircraft. He never enjoyed the cramped working conditions anyway.

Eddie's first break came soon after he joined the American Guild of Variety Artists (AGVA) in 1946 and, with the war over, Americans were champing at the bit to return to normalcy. One company with big ideas was Mercury Records, which had acquired a stable of musical artists

The 17-Inch Baseball Bat

such as Tony Martin, Patti Page, Frankie Lane, and many other top-notch performers. The owners of the company decided they needed some sort of gimmick to push their name and their sales. The company "borrowed" an idea from Philip Morris Cigarettes and created a "living logo" character called "Mercury Man."

According to a clipping from an Advertising Magazine, "The newest promotional stunt in the record field is a take-off on Philip Morris's "Johnny" gimmick. Mercury Records has hired a "Mercury Man," a 3-foot, 7-inch midget. The twenty year old Mercury man's real name is Eddie Gaedel and he will be used primarily to contact disk jockeys, to autograph Mercury disks at department and retail stores when they are released, to put in personal appearances at Mercury distributors throughout the country, and to appear at places where Mercury attractions are being featured."

"Much of Mercury's future promotion will be tied around Mercury Man and a contest will be held through record stores and counters to give him a surname. Life-sized cutouts are being made and will be displayed in Mercury distributor's windows and on show counters throughout the country. The Mercury Man is garbed in an aluminum-winged helmet, winged boots, a red cape, and red trousers."

"Mercury execs added that he will be used as a central character in a series of kid albums also. Mercury Man bowed into his promotional

The 17-Inch Baseball Bat

role by giving away 150 records nightly at the College Inn Nightery, where Buddy Rich is currently appearing."

It was unfortunate that the gig with Mercury Records failed to produce the desired results. Whether it was due to lack of receptive enthusiasm by the public, lack of follow through by the company's management, or simply due to Eddie's quirks is an unanswerable question. It did not help that Eddie was continually complaining about having to travel by himself, without a company representative to accompany him. In the end, the venture failed and Mercury Man turned out to be more like Lead Man. Eddie turned in his uniform and winged shoes, opting to stay in Chicago.

Beginning in 1948, Eddie obtained employment as a waiter at The Midget Club in Chicago. The establishment would become one of the touchstones of his life in Chicago where he worked off-and-on until his death in 1961.

Parnell St. Aubin and his wife, Mary Ellen, owned the eatery and bar. Parnell, unlike Eddie, actually did play one of the Munchkins in "The Wizard of Oz," but parts for little folks were few and far between in Tinsel Town so he returned to his hometown of Chicago where he married Mary Ellen. They met in the toy department of Goldblatt's Department Store when they were both working as Santa's Elves during the Christmas season.

Like a lot of midgets, they were disappointed

The 17-Inch Baseball Bat

that most businesses failed to understand the "social needs" of midget clientele. Parnell and Mary Ellen wanted to create a Dining Lounge that would cater to and "fit" little people like themselves.

In 1948, The Midget Club opened its doors at 6356 South Kedzie Street and it became an instant success—it was the place to see and be seen. The club had a downsized bar counter, along with downsized bar stools, tables, and chairs. Only little people could sit and enjoy an adult beverage without being crammed into the small spaces. It was impossible for a "normal" sized person to sit at the bar, but they could sit at one of the "regular" sized tables and chairs in the joint. Signed photos of Munchkin Parnell with Judy Garland and Ray Bolger graced the wall next to the bar counter. Eddie was still employed at the club at the time of his death in 1961. The club stayed open until 1982, when both Parnell and Mary Ellen had passed away.

In 1951, Eddie's once-in-a-lifetime break came out of the blue. Bill Veeck, who had purchased the St. Louis Browns just two months earlier, decided he needed a very special publicity stunt.

His plan was to hire a midget as a pinch-hitter in the second game of the August 19 doubleheader against the Detroit Tigers. A number of little men were brought to him and they were all deemed to be "insufficient" to his needs so he explained his situation to Bob Fishel, the team's

The 17-Inch Baseball Bat

publicity man. He said, "There is a difference between a midget and a dwarf. A dwarf has a genetic disorder and his limbs are shorter in comparison to his body than a midget. A midget is perfectly formed but simply a small person. I want a midget."

Finally, with the aid of an AGVA agent, Veeck settled on Eddie Gaedel, whose appearance was part of a promotion for both the American League and the Falstaff brewing company which was owned by the Griesedieck Brothers brewery in St. Louis. The year 1951 was the 50th anniversary of the American League so Veeck also claimed it was the 50th anniversary of Falstaff, too. He never let the truth get in the way of a good story.

According to Veeck, August 19 would be a day of "miniatures." He would give miniature orchids to all the ladies and he would give all ticket holders a set of miniature Falstaff beer bottle salt-and-pepper shakers.

The whole pinch-hitting performance lasted perhaps ten or fifteen minutes and then Eddie returned to the dugout, made his way to the showers, and dressed himself before heading for the Press Box for an interview.

It brings to mind the "The Gunfight at the O.K. Corral" which lasted no more than 30 to 45 seconds but managed to create the legend of Wyatt Earp.

Immediately after his ground-breaking gig as "The Littlest Brownie" in 1951, Eddie had

The 17-Inch Baseball Bat

more offers than he could handle. Still connected with AGVA, they obtained work for him and he made appearances on the Ed Sullivan Show, the Bing Crosby Show, and various radio shows. Radio was still an important entertainment medium at that time. Eddie made almost $20,000 in 1951 but he failed to follow up and take advantage of his new celebrity status.

People who were close to Eddie said he simply couldn't handle his short-lived brush with fame and fortune. Eddie suffered from a combination of a bad temper coupled with a severe drinking problem. One person from The Midget Club who knew him said quite frankly, "He was a belligerent little drunk. Period."

That, in fact, was a bad thing for a midget. He would start fights with normal sized guys and get the snot knocked out of him, then he'd come back for more until he couldn't stand up.

A couple of weeks after his appearance in St. Louis, Eddie was in Cincinnati for a personal appearance at a rodeo and that evening he was stopped by a policeman for spewing obscenities at people on the street. He tried, and failed, to convince the officer he was a major league baseball player and ended up in jail for the night.

According to Bill Veeck's wife, Frances, "Eddie became quite the hero—in his own mind—and when he began to drink, his inebriated ego took over his entire personality. When Eddie was full of liquor, he was also full of himself."

Veeck said of Eddie, "It got to be that the

The 17-Inch Baseball Bat

only time Eddie was happy was when he was bombed outta his skull. When he got a few drinks in him, he thought he was six-foot-nine."

Eddie could have made the big-time if he had only handled himself better. He was offered motion-picture work in California, a well-paying job with Buster Brown Shoes, and the Oscar Meyer company wanted to make him a "living logo" for their products. Unlike Mercury Records, Oscar Meyer knew what they were doing and they would have made Eddie a very wealthy and well-known man. They were also willing to accommodate his eccentricities.

Regarding the motion-picture opportunity, Eddie's mother said he told her, "Mom, I'm not going to California alone. I don't know anyone out there and it's no life being locked up in a room by myself." She said, "He was always scared to go out." Eddie refused to go and the studio never called back.

The Buster Brown thing was a little better, but not by much. He agreed to work with them and appear as the Buster Brown Character, but only in the Chicago area at specific store locations. He made a couple of appearances and the company never called back.

The Oscar Meyer company really wanted to hire him and they were willing to deal with all of his complaints and idiosyncrasies. They offered to have a person travel with him, help him with the appearances, and even help him with his alcohol consumption. It would have been perfect,

The 17-Inch Baseball Bat

but, once again, even though they would accommodate him and his foibles, Eddie told them, "No, it's just too much travel. I don't like to travel. I can't travel that much." Frustrated, the company said, "Okay," thanked him for his time, and the project was dropped. They never called back, either.

A month after the "Littlest Brownie" gig, Eddie made an appearance at Sycamore, Illinois for a healthy fee. Two amateur teams were playing that day and Gaedel was playing for the Sycamore Sons, a team formed in 1925. This time, Gaedel was allowed to swing his bat and at his single appearance at the plate he struck out. Unlike Bob "Sugar" Cain of the Detroit Tigers, the rival pitcher, Gene Davis, managed to pitch with a low arc and got the ball over the plate and into the strike zone. Gaedel swung at one pitch and two more were called strikes by the umpire. Gaedel jumped out of the batter's box at both rulings and began to harangue the umpire, saying, "You're nuts! You're the worst umpire I ever want to see!"

Witnessing this was a ten-year-old batboy named Morrie McPherson who said, "I think the the by-play with the umpire was part of an act. I think Gaedel just wanted to get the job done and get out of there. He acted like he was happy to get it over with and be on his way back to the dugout."

McPherson was able to obtain Eddie's autograph just before he left and he has kept it all

The 17-Inch Baseball Bat

his life. He has no intention of selling it. "I'm just a collector, I never sell anything," he says.

Two days after batting in Sycamore, Gaedel was supposed to be the Grand Marshal for the Elburn Days Parade (in northern Illinois) but he arrived too late to participate. After the parade, a game was played by two local teams of teenagers—sponsored by the American Legion—and although Gaedel didn't play in the field (he never owned a baseball glove), he was allowed to bat three times. He suffered two strikeouts and earned a walk to first base, but he never advanced nor scored during the game. Kenny Johnson, the opposing pitcher, picked Gaedel off at first base when Gaedel took too much of a lead toward second.

Following those months of fame, things slowed down for Eddie and people forgot about him. On rare occasions he would get a phone call from an agent with an offer for an appearance that paid a decent sum. In spite of his reluctance to travel, Eddie ended up having to travel to make it to these gigs in circuses, rodeos, store openings, and other second rate entertainment venues.

Frank Saucier, the baseball player for whom Eddie had been a pinch-hitter in 1951 remembered, "I had been recalled into the Navy during the Korean War and I was stationed in Pensacola, Florida. I heard the little guy had taken a job as a clown with the Ringling Brothers and Barnum & Bailey Circus."

The 17-Inch Baseball Bat

Saucier said Eddie told him he had taken the job because he was never alone. He was surrounded by other midgets and they all kept pretty tight together. He said he felt safe.

Eddie stayed in contact with Veeck and he appeared in a couple of White Sox games when Veeck returned to Comiskey Park. On May 26, 1959, Gaedel and three other midgets "landed" in a helicopter at Comiskey Park dressed as Martians and carrying Ray Guns. The Martians ran to the dugout, "captured" diminutive middle infielders Nellie Fox and Luis Aparicio, and escorted them to home plate for a special ceremony. On April 19, 1961, just two months before Eddie's death, Gaedel and seven other midgets were hired to work as Box Seat vendors after Veeck heard complaints that the usual vendors were too tall and were blocking the view of the fans. The little guys all quit after the game, however, saying the job was too hard on their feet.

Sadly, Eddie had suffered a lot during his childhood, being the target of teasing and outright bullying. He became very self-conscious and even as a child he displayed anger at being so small. His mother remembers him as often being scared to go to school and he disliked leaving his home.

The thing was that, in spite of the obstacles life had put in his way, Eddie was never, ever a coward, and he refused to back down from his abusers. Many times a tormentor was surprised to find that Eddie would most certainly fight

The 17-Inch Baseball Bat

back, socking the crap out of the bully who started it.

Learning that he would, indeed, defend himself, small groups of children would gang up on him, even after he had graduated from high school. Eddie's mother remembered that one such group was made up of little kids between five and ten years old. His mother said, "When Eddie hauled off and socked a couple of the kids, their mothers called the police and complained—and it was Eddie they arrested and threw into a cell for the night. The police said since he was an adult, he was responsible." When Eddie threatened to take the matter to court, however, the children's mothers decided to drop the matter.

Eddie's sister, Rosa, said, "He was a happy-go-lucky guy on the outside, but he was really suffering on the inside. He had an extra rough time in grade school. He'd come home crying and swearing. The teachers wouldn't do anything about it, either."

Put all of this together—a lifetime of teasing, bullying, threats, and intimidation—and it's little wonder that Eddie grew up the way he did. All of the collective abuse contributed to a growing insecurity due to his size, creating a thoroughly combative stance against anyone he believed had slighted, ridiculed, or mocked him.

His anxiety also grew unabated throughout his life when it came to being away from home, making him hesitant to travel or to be away

The 17-Inch Baseball Bat

from his "comfort zone" for any length of time. Although he forced himself to take jobs when his financial situation demanded such activity, it was it was always with a great deal of reluctance.

During the last years of his life, Eddie lived with his indigent mother and brother in an apartment on the South-side of Chicago. Eddie was fond of his mother and she reciprocated the feelings, always worrying about him when he was away from home.

By the start of the 1960s, Eddie's health was failing due to extreme high blood pressure and an enlarged heart. His mother reported during an interview that he would simply get dizzy, pass out, and fall down on many occasions. Of course, the continued habit of heavy drinking compounded the issue.

On June 18, 1961, Eddie was unemployed and, using what meager funds he had, he went to the local bowling alley where he proceeded to get drunk. As usual, once the alcohol took over, he became belligerent and started bothering the other patrons of the ten pins. Finally, the manager told him he would have to leave.

Apparently some of the guys he had insulted followed him home and gave him a severe beating near his apartment. They also took his last $11 out of his wallet. At this point, there is some confusion about exactly when and how Eddie died.

The most prevalent story, which has been

The 17-Inch Baseball Bat

printed and repeated most often is that he came home after the beating, had climbed into bed, and his mother found him the next morning—dead. These reports also indicate bruises around his legs and knees as well as on the left side of his face. Newspaper reports of the incident indicated that an inquest was scheduled, but no newspaper reports can be found relating the specific findings of such an inquest. It's thought that Eddie died from a heart attack induced by the beating he had received at the hands of unknown assailants.

The other story comes directly from Eddie's mother, Helen Gadele. In an interview for the August 21, 1971 issue of the Louisville, Kentucky "Courier-Journal" Mrs. Gaedele recalls, "I was waiting up for him. I remember it was on a Sunday. He was usually home by 9 o'clock. He wasn't one to stay out late and I wondered what had happened to him. I couldn't sleep."

"All of a sudden my door chimes rang and I was afraid to open the door. I asked, 'Who is it?' It was the police. Two officers had brought Eddie home. They said they found him at 47th and Wolcott laying on the curb. He was all beat up something awful. Eddie told them he had eleven dollars in his wallet and that was it was taken from him."

"A little fellow like that. He never harmed anybody. I couldn't get over it. That happened sometime in January, I remember. A few months later, he was dead. He had just turned 36 years

The 17-Inch Baseball Bat

old. He died in my arms. My little boy, Eddie, died in my arms. He was a very good boy. He'd say to people, 'My mother is at home all alone and I don't want her to be alone.' Now Eddie's gone and I'm engulfed in loneliness."

Eddie's funeral attracted about 50 people. The only former ballplayer in attendance was Bob Cain, who had long since retired from baseball. Cain and Gaedel struck up a friendship of sorts since their face-off and they had exchanged Christmas cards until Gaedel's death. Cain and his wife drove over 300 miles to pay their respects to his former opponent. In a 1989 interview, Cain said, "I never even met him, but I felt obligated to go. It kind of threw me for a loop that no other baseball people were there."

Cain kept the prayer card from Gaedel's funeral mass. Its concluding words still seem apropos for Eddie Gaedel. It reads, "Merciful Savior, send Thy angels to conduct Thy departed servant to a place of refreshment, light, and peace. Amen."

Bill Veeck said he would have attended the funeral, but he was in the middle of cancer treatment at the time.

36-year-old Eddie Gaedel was interred at Saint Mary Catholic Cemetery and Mausoleum in Cook County, Illinois.

Some years later, a group calling themselves the "Honor the Midget Committee" sent letters to the Postmaster General of the United States along with several artist's designs requesting an

The 17-Inch Baseball Bat

"Eddie Gaedel stamp." The proposal was rejected.

The 17-Inch Baseball Bat

Eddie's ready for his first communion.
He's a handsome little lad.

The 17-Inch Baseball Bat

The newspaper where Eddie worked
when he was in high school.

The 17-Inch Baseball Bat

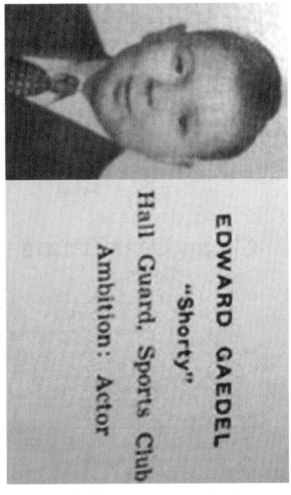

Eddie's High School picture and personal information.

EDWARD GAEDEL
"Shorty"
Hall Guard, Sports Club
Ambition: Actor

The 17-Inch Baseball Bat

"Mercury Man!" Eddie's first important gig as the mascot of Mercury Records. Boots, buttons, and wings all polished and ready for anything!

The 17-Inch Baseball Bat

Mercury Records label. The little man was from a caricature of Eddie drawn by a commercial artist.

The 17-Inch Baseball Bat

Eddie giving some highly personal service to the ladies at "The Midget Club" in Chicago. Eddie appreciated a well turned ankle and the ladies liked him, too.

The 17-Inch Baseball Bat

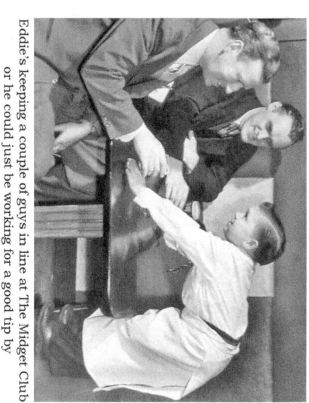

Eddie's keeping a couple of guys in line at The Midget Club or he could just be working for a good tip by telling "baseball stories."

The 17-Inch Baseball Bat

Eddie helping the 1952 White Sox with some
publicity photos after they won the
American League pennant. It's a
good close up of both Eddie
and his "Thunder Bat."

⅛ — Gaedel	8 — B. Taylor, if
2 — Marsh, if	9 — Lollar, c
3 — Arft. if	10 — Batts, c
5 — Young, if	11 — Maguire, if
6 — Jennings, if	12 — Wood, of

A cutting from the official scorecard for the
second game of the double-header on
August 19, 1951 in Sportsman's Park.

The 17-Inch Baseball Bat

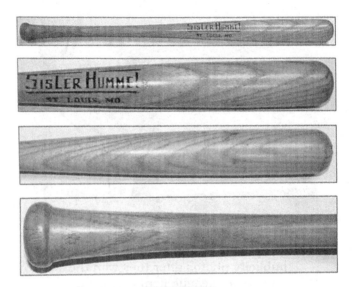

Eddie's Bat:
17-inches, 23-ounces.

Details:
Full Bat.
Front Barrel.
Back Barrel.
Handle.
Knob.

The 17-Inch Baseball Bat

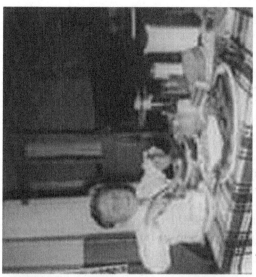

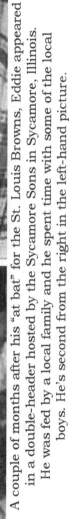

A couple of months after his "at bat" for the St. Louis Browns, Eddie appeared in a double-header hosted by the Sycamore Sons in Sycamore, Illinois. He was fed by a local family and he spent time with some of the local boys. He's second from the right in the left-hand picture.

The 17-Inch Baseball Bat

On May 26, 1959, Gaedel and three other "Martians" landed in Comiskey Park. With their Ray Guns, they captured diminutive infielders Nellie Fox and Luis Apparico, escorting them to home plate for a special ceremony. Eddie is at the microphone.

The 17-Inch Baseball Bat

Eddie Gaedel's St. Louis Browns uniform on display in the Baseball Hall of Fame.

The 17-Inch Baseball Bat

4801 S. Wolcott Avenue; The apartment house in which Eddie Gaedel died. He and his mother lived upstairs.

The 17-Inch Baseball Bat

Eddie and his parents. Carl served in WWI and was 39 when Eddie was born. Helen was 24 when Eddie was born.

The 17-Inch Baseball Bat

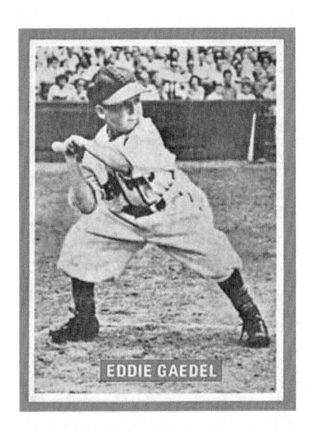

The 17-Inch Baseball Bat

EDWARD CARL GAEDEL
Born 6-8-25, Chicago, Ill   Died 6-18-61, Chicago, Ill
Hgt. 3'7"   Wgt. 65   Batted Right   Threw Left

Eddie made top baseball headlines in August of 1951, when he was sent up to pinch hit. As part of a promotional stunt to help the Brown's attendance, the midget made his only batting appearance against the Tigers and walked on four pitches. He was then taken out of the game in favor of a pinch runner and midgets were banned from participating in any more big league baseball contests. Thus Eddie has become the smallest man in baseball history.

MAJOR LEAGUE BATTING RECORD

YEAR	TEAM	LEA.	G	AB	R	H	2B	3B	HR	RBI	AVE.
1951	St. L.	AL	1	0	0	0	0	0	0	0	.000

The 17-Inch Baseball Bat

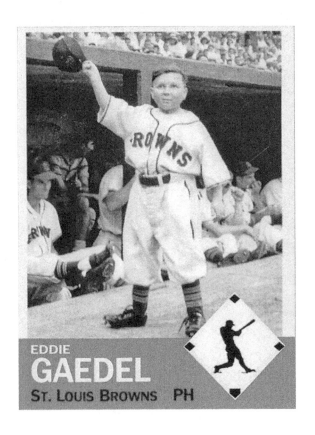

The 17-Inch Baseball Bat

EDDIE GAEDEL
1951 St. Louis Browns – Pinch Hitter

Ht: 3-7 Wt: 65 Bats: Right Throws: Right
Born: June 8, 1925 Home: Chicago, Illinois

After just one trip to the plate last season, Eddie was banned by American League President Will Harridge, and his contract declared void.
When Gaedel strode to the plate as a pinch hitter on August 19th against the Detroit Tigers at St. Louis, veteran umpire Ed Hurley was dumbfounded, and stopped the game. To his disbelief, he was shown Eddie's contract, and play was resumed. Opposing pitcher Bob Cain, unable to throw a strike into a 2 inch strike zone, walked Gaedel on 4 pitches. Eddie was then replaced by a pinch runner!

18

Ed was the shortest player in major league baseball last season. The tallest big league player was nearly 3 feet taller than Gaedel. Who was he?

Cubs first baseman Chuck Connors at 6-6

Diamond Collection   MCP © 2009

The 17-Inch Baseball Bat

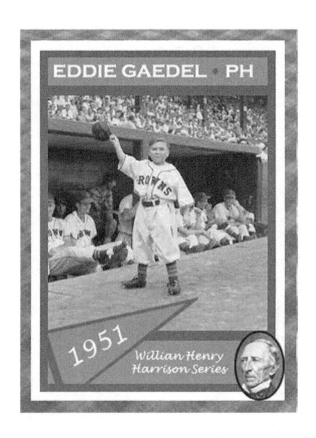

The 17-Inch Baseball Bat

WHH 2	EDDIE GAEDEL											PH
COMPLETE MAJOR LEAGUE BATTING RECORD												
YR	TEAM	G	AB	R	H	2B	3B	HR	RBI	SB	CS	BB	SO	OBP	AVG
'51 BROWNS	1	0	0	0	0	0	0	0	0	0	1	0	1.000	.000
MAJ. LEA. TOTALS	1	0	0	0	0	0	0	0	0	0	1	0	1.000	.000

- Signed by the St. Louis Browns owner Bill Veeck as an amateur free agent on 08/19/1951, the same day he made his major league debut.
- Wore uniform number 1/8 and was the only ball player to ever have have dwarfism.
- Pinch hit for Browns lead off hitter, Frank Saucier, to start game two of a double header and walked in his only plate appearance.
- Had his contract voided by the league two days after he signed on 08/21/1951.

RANDOM BASEBALL FACT
Cap Anson, Albert Belle, Ken Griffey Jr., Reggie Jackson, Kirby Puckett and Babe Ruth have all had candy bars named after them.

HT: 3'7" WT: 65 BATS: RIGHT THROWS: LEFT DOB: 06/08/1925
MLB DEBUT: 08/19/1951 FINAL MLB GAME: 08/19/1951

WFC Custom Card Productions©

The 17-Inch Baseball Bat

The 17-Inch Baseball Bat

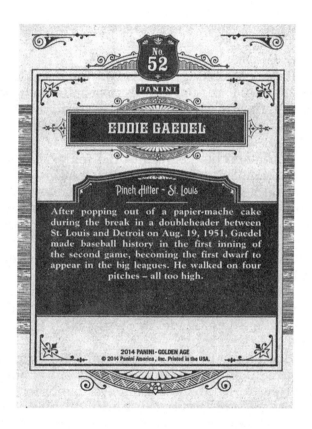

The 17-Inch Baseball Bat

Bob Cain

Robert Max (Sugar) Cain was born on October 16, 1924 in Longford, Kansas. He died on April 8, 1997 in Cleveland, Ohio at the age of 72.

He batted and threw the baseball left-handed.

Bob made his debut into the major leagues on September 18, 1948 with the Chicago White Sox and his final appearance was also with the White Sox on September 11, 1954. In between his time with the White Sox, he played for the Detroit Tigers and the St. Louis Browns.

His win-loss record was 37-44 respectively, with an ERA of 4.50, and 249 strikeouts.

Bob's most notable appearance on the mound was when he three four straight balls past little Eddie Gaedel in Sportsman's Park in 1951.

Bob originally signed with the New York Giants in 1943 and he threw a shut out against the New York Yankees in his first major league appearance in 1949. On April 23, 1952, he matched one-hitters with the great Bob Feller and won (1-0) at Sportsman's Park in St. Louis.

For his part in the Eddie Gaedel extravaganza, Bob remembered, "I went to the mound to

The 17-Inch Baseball Bat

start to pitch the bottom half of the first inning and as I was warming up, Eddie came out of the dugout, picked up three little bats, and started swinging them around as though he was warming up. Swift and I couldn't understand what was going on until the little guy headed for the plate. When he was in his crouch, his strikezone couldn't have been more than an inch-and-a-half. It was nuts."

Bob Swift, Cain's catcher told him to, "Keep it low, Bob."

"I couldn't stop laughing," Bob said.

Nearby observers related the opinion that, "Cain was laughing so hard at the prospect of pitching to Gaedel that he practically fell of the mound with every pitch."

After four straight balls, Bob just stood there, shaking his head and watching Gaedel saunter toward first base.

Bob played in 150 major league games, with 140 appearances as pitcher, for a total of 628 innings.

Bob and his wife drove over 300 miles to show their respects at Eddie Gaedel's funeral in 1961. Bob was the only ballplayer who showed up.

After leaving baseball, he and his wife lived in Euclid, Ohio for the remaining 40 years of his life. He died of cancer at the age of 72.

The 17-Inch Baseball Bat

The 17-Inch Baseball Bat

BOB CAIN
Pitcher—Detroit Tigers
Born: Longford, Kan., Oct. 16, 1924
Height: 6 ft. Weight: 165
Bats: Left Throws: Left

As a rookie with the 1950 Sox Bob appeared in 34 games. Won 9, lost 12. Had a 3.92 earned run average. Signed a contract with Giants after receiving offers from 8 major league clubs. Entered military service shortly afterward. With Manchester, New England League, 1946. Won 13 while losing 4. The White Sox bought his contract, September 1949. Traded to Detroit Tigers, May 1951.

No. 197 in the 1951 SERIES

BASEBALL
PICTURE CARDS
©1951 Bowman Gum, Inc., Phila., Pa., U.S.A.

The 17-Inch Baseball Bat

Hope your target in the future is better than mine was in 1951.

Bob & Judy Cain

Bob "Sugar" Cain's Christmas Card for 1951 (Front)

The 17-Inch Baseball Bat

Bob "Sugar" Cain's Christmas Card for 1951 (Inside)

The 17-Inch Baseball Bat

Bob Swift

Robert Virgil Swift was born on March 5, 1915 in Salina, Kansas. A right-hander, Bob made his debut in the major leagues on April 16, 1940 for the St. Louis Browns. His final appearance was on September 27, 1963, playing and coaching for the Detroit Tigers.

Throughout his career, he played for the St. Louis Browns, the Philadelphia Athletics, and the Detroit Tigers.

Bob earned his World Series ring when the Detroit Tigers took the championship from the Chicago Cubs in 1945 with a 4-3 record.

Bob appeared in 1,001 games, had a batting record of .231, with 14 home runs, and 238 runs batted in. His 635 hits included 86 doubles, 3 triples, and 14 home runs.

When Bob stopped playing baseball, he started coaching for the Tigers, the Kansas City Athletics, and the Washington Senators.

Bob was made acting manager of the Tigers when Chuck Dressen suffered his second heart attack during spring training.

Under Bob's leadership, the Tigers had a record of 32-25, but during that time, he was hospitalized with what was thought to be food pois-

The 17-Inch Baseball Bat

oning. Tests, however, revealed that Bob was suffering from advanced and inoperable lung cancer. Three months later, on October 17, 1966, he died in Detroit at the age of 51.

His record as interim manager with the Tigers in 1965-66 was 56-43 (.566) and his entire career record as a manger was 69-43 (.605) which is pretty darn good.

The 17-Inch Baseball Bat

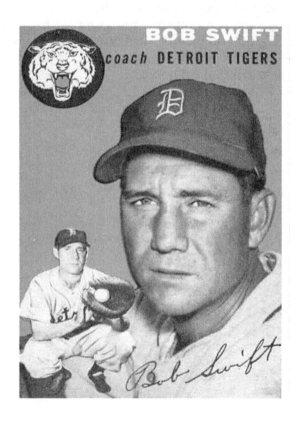

The 17-Inch Baseball Bat

The 17-Inch Baseball Bat

Jim Delsing

James Henry Delsing was born on November 13, 1925 in Rudolph, Wisconsin and he died in Chesterfield, Missouri, on May 4, 2006 at the age of 80.

He was one of those fellows who batted left-handed, but threw the ball right-handed. The proper name for such a person is "cross dominant" but according to my Grandpa, he had "hand confusion."

Jim made his major league debut on April 21, 1948 with the Chicago White Sox and his final appearance was on September 30, 1960, playing for the Kansas City Athletics.

Jim's batting average was .255 with 40 home runs and 286 runs batted in.

During his career of 822 games over 10 seasons, he played for the Chicago White Sox, New York Yankees, St. Louis Browns, Detroit Tigers, and Kansas City Athletics.

Jim started in baseball quite young, signing his first professional contract at the age of 16 with the Green Bay Bluejays in the Wisconsin State League. He left baseball after two years to join the U. S. Army Medical Corps, serving in Europe during World War II. He resumed his

The 17-Inch Baseball Bat

baseball career in 1946 and made his major league debut with the White Sox in 1948.

Jim led the American League left fielders with a .996 fielding percentage in 1954, but his batting average began to slip and in 1955 he lost playing time to Charlie Maxwell.

Starting in 1957, he played three seasons in the minor leagues and he was on the Charleston Senators team when they won the American Association League pennant in 1958.

In 1960, after several of the Athletics outfielders suffered injuries, Jim was brought onto their roster for the remainder of the season. The next season, Jim finished his professional career by playing 16 games for Kansas City.

When he played with the Browns, Jim came to like the St. Louis area and resided there for the rest of his life.

Following his retirement from the "spheroid game" and tossing around the old "ellipsoid of revolution," Jim worked as an advertising salesman for the "St. Louis Review" for over thirty years. He gave his time as a volunteer to local Catholic Charities, and he participated in the St. Louis Browns Fan Club which continues to rejoice in the history and remembrance of "The Brownies."

Jim died of cancer on May 4, 2006.

The 17-Inch Baseball Bat

The 17-Inch Baseball Bat

JIM DELSING

Outfield—St. Louis Browns
Born: Rudolph, Wis., Nov. 13, 1925
Height: 5-10½   Weight: 175
Bats: Left   Throws: Right

After knocking off a .400 average in 12 games for the Yankees in 1950, Jim was traded to the Browns. He took part in 69 games for St. Louis, hitting .263. In 1949 he hit .317 for the Yankees' Kansas City farm team, and .350 in 9 games for the parent club. Began as a shortstop and switched to the outfield the next season. Voted the best outfielder in the American Association.

No. 279 in the 1951 SERIES

BASEBALL

PICTURE CARDS

©1951 Bowman Gum, Inc., Phila., Pa., U.S.A.

The 17-Inch Baseball Bat

Frank Saucier

Francis Field Saucier was born on May 28, 1926 in Leslie, Missouri. As of the writing of this book, he is said to be alive and well at the age of 94 and living in Amarillo, Texas

Frank was another ballplayer who had "hand confusion" batting left-handed and throwing right-handed.

He made his debut in the major leagues with the St. Louis Browns on July 21, 1951. His final appearance was for the St. Louis Browns on September 23, 1951.

His batting average was .071, home runs were 0, and runs batted in were 1. All were accomplished with the St. Louis Browns.

Although Frank was named the Minor League Player of the Year for the San Antonio Missions team in 1951, his major league career as an outfielder only lasted for two months in 1951.

Frank played a total of 18 games with the Browns and had one hit in 14 times at bat, hence his .071 batting average. He also had three walks, scored four runs, and had a single RBI.

His minor league career had shown much

The 17-Inch Baseball Bat

more promise. He hit .348 in his first professional season (1941) in the Illinois State League and he followed up the next year with a .446 batting average at Wichita Falls in (1949).

Unfortunately, he suffered a severe shoulder injury in 1951 and then he was re-drafted as a Lieutenant into the U.S. Navy during the Korean War—he was just one of many World War II "retreads" brought back for Korean War duty. A number of careers were destroyed by the U.S. Government in this manner.

With his baseball career ruined, Frank attended and graduated from Westminster College in Fulton, Missouri garnering degrees in both math and physics. It's the same college where Winston Churchill gave his historic speech denouncing the Soviet Union and its "Iron Curtain" across eastern Europe.

Frank remembered quite well the day he was taken out of the game and replaced by a pinch-hitter named Eddie Gaedel.

Frank says, "I shouldn't have been in the game to begin with. I was suffering from acute bursitis in my right shoulder and I couldn't even swing a bat. Nor could I thrown a ball without extreme pain. I had been undergoing treatment for my shoulder and on Sunday morning Zack Taylor, our manager, told me I was starting in right field. It was right field, not center, as Veeck wrote in his book. I couldn't understand it because I hadn't played in a couple of weeks, but I thought, 'Well, we'll just see where this goes.' "

The 17-Inch Baseball Bat

"As I started to the plate, Zack said to me, 'No, wait a minute, we've got a pinch-hitter.' I looked around and here comes Eddie, with three miniature bats on his shoulder."

"I just laughed. I thought this was one of the greatest acts of show business I'd ever seen, and still do. But the umpire didn't. It was Ed Hurley, and he said to Taylor, 'You can't do this.' And Zack said, 'Yes, I can, I have the contract right here in my pocket.' "

"I remember Zack hollering to Eddie, 'Don't swing!' So Eddie bent over and his strike zone was about an inch high. He walked on four pitches, of course. As he trotted to first base, he stopped and tipped his hat to the crowd and waved and then when he got on first, Jim Delsing went out to pinch-run for him. Eddie came back to the dugout and sat down beside me. I said, 'Eddie, you were kind of showin' it up a little bit there, weren't you?' 'Man,' he said, 'I felt like Babe Root.' "

"Contrary to what some folks have written, I've never felt bad about being pinch-hit for by a midget because I probably should never have been with the Browns to begin with."

"I was making more as the leading hitter in the Texas League with San Antonio than I would have made as a rookie in the major leagues, so I was content."

"I had invested in an oil well, and in February of 1951, lo and behold, the well began flowing 150 barrels a day, so I quit baseball."

The 17-Inch Baseball Bat

"Bill Veeck called me in July and said he wanted to see me. We talked all through the night, with him trying to persuade me to play with the Browns and I finally gave in."

"He was on crutches, and before he left I asked him, 'What are you doing on those crutches?'"

He said, "Well, I got shot in the leg on Guadalcanal."

(This wasn't exactly true. Bill was injured when an artillery piece misfired and smashed his foot, putting a large gash in it).

Frank said, "Don't you have a false foot?"

Bill answered, "Yes, I do, but I'll tell you something," and he chuckled as he said, "When I go to make a deal and my position isn't strong, I go on crutches. When I'm in the drivers seat during a deal, then I wear my false foot."

During his Korean War duty, Frank was stationed at Pensacola, Florida where he heard that Eddie was working as a clown.

Frank remembered, "My wife and I went to the Ringling Brothers and Barnum & Bailey Circus when they came to town and I saw Eddie come tumbling out of one of those tiny cars full of midget clowns. After the show, I found him and we talked for a few minutes. He was really happy to see me and he reminisced about us being 'old teammates.' I asked how he was getting along, and he said, 'Well, it ain't baseball, but it's a livin.'"

The 17-Inch Baseball Bat

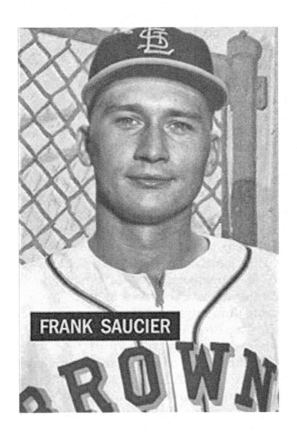

The 17-Inch Baseball Bat

FRANK SAUCIER

Outfield—St. Louis Browns
Born: Leslie, Mo., May 28, 1926
Height: 6-1 Weight: 180
Bats: Left Throws: Right

Brownies' fans eagerly await Frank's debut at Sportsman's Park. They have been following his rapid rise in the St. Louis farm system for the past three seasons. In Class D ball in 1948, he hit .357. He made the jump to Class B in 1949 and led all of professional baseball with a .446 average. Last season his .343 mark led the Texas League. He appears to be ready to face big league pitching.

No. 326 in the 1951 SERIES

BASEBALL
PICTURE CARDS

© 2012 Bobman Gum, Inc., Iola., Wis., U.S.A.

The 17-Inch Baseball Bat

Zack Taylor

James Wren "Zack" Taylor was born on July 27, 1898 and he died on September 19, 1974. Zack was a player, coach, scout, and manager during his baseball years.

He played Major League Baseball as a catcher for the Brooklyn Robins, Boston Braves, New York Giants, and Chicago Cubs.

During his 16 year major league career, Zack played in 918 games, had 748 hits in 2,865 times at bat, and ended up with a .261 batting average. He had 9 home runs, 311 runs batted in, and an on-base percentage of .304. At the end of his career, he posted a .977 fielding percentage.

Zack was known for his "defensive abilities" as a catcher and he had a lengthy career behind the plate in spite of not being a powerful hitter. When his playing career ended, he became the manager for the St. Louis Browns. In total, his career lasted for 58 years—a long time in baseball.

Zack joined the St. Louis Browns as a coach in 1941 and was a member of the team during the "Street Car Series" in 1944 between the Browns and the Cardinals.

The 17-Inch Baseball Bat

Zack was manager of the Browns on that fateful day when Bill Veeck instructed him to have Eddie's Gaedel's signed contract on hand if the home base umpire complained about a midget being a pinch-hitter.

Zack was also present for another Veeck baseball stunt called "Grandstand Managers Night."

More than 1,000 placards were handed out to "Grandstand Managers" who paid to sit in a special section behind the Browns dugout. Using cards reading "Yes" or "No" the fans voted on key game decisions.

Zack "took the night off" and sat in a rocking chair, wearing casual clothing, and smoking his pipe while the game was played.

The Browns won the game.

The 17-Inch Baseball Bat

The 17-Inch Baseball Bat

ZACK TAYLOR

Manager—St. Louis Browns
Born: Yulee, Fla., July 27, 1898
Height: 5-11½   Weight: 180
Batted: Right   Threw: Right

Entered baseball in 1915, and played through 1937. Made a brief comeback in 1940, catching 4 games for the Toledo Mudhens. Clubs for which Zack played in the majors were the Dodgers, Braves, Giants, Cubs and Yankees. Had first experience as a manager with Allentown in 1935. First piloted the Browns in Aug., 1946. A coach for the Pirates in 1947. Again took over reins, St. Louis, '48.

No. 315 in the 1951 SERIES

BASEBALL

PICTURE CARDS

©1951 Bowman Gum, Inc., Phila., Pa., U.S.A.

The 17-Inch Baseball Bat

Chapter Five

Midgets of Note:
Baseball & Otherwise.

According to the various legends and fables within the boundaries of Baseball Shiredom, a total of two midgets have played in professional, major league games. The first would be the fictitious "Pearl du Monville" who was the imaginary little guy invented by the mind of author, humorist, and artist James Thurber. In his 1941 story named "You Could Look It Up" Thurber has his character (which sounds a lot like the real life Billy Barty) create havoc upon the baseball diamond of the St. Louis Squawks, managed by a fellow who is reminiscent of Casey Stengel in both his language and his decisions.

In short, the story is a complete hoot and well worth a detailed reading. A quick summation is that with a count of 3 and 0, Pearl, with visions of the next day's headlines flashing through his mind, swings his toothpick bat with all the might his 35-inch frame can muster. The result is a dribbler in front of the plate. The catcher kicks it; the pitcher falls on his face; and the shortstop stumbles. There's still time, how-

The 17-Inch Baseball Bat

ever, for the second baseman to pick up the ball and fire to first. Pearl is out by 10 feet and the game is over. Then all hell breaks loose! It will be left to the reader to ferret out and enjoy this wonderful baseball story.

The second midget of note would be the famous 3-foot, 7-inch figure of Eddie Gaedel, the pinch-hitter for Frank Saucier with Bill Veeck's St. Louis Browns in 1951. The account of Gaedel's legend is accounted for in this book as well as in other baseball literature.

The purpose of this chapter will be to rectify two glaring errors in relation to baseball's history of midgets and their accomplishments.

It must be admitted that some nit-picking is required concerning all of these reportages. Firstly, as previously mentioned, "Pearl du Monville" is a fictional character. Secondly, Eddie Gaedel was not the first midget to play in a professional baseball game, as is often claimed. Gaedel is actually the first (and only) midget to have played in a professional "major league" game.

There are two other midgets who have played in baseball games. One of them played a professional game in the minor leagues and the other played in a high school game in Rhode Island.

The 17-Inch Baseball Bat

Jerry D. Sullivan

The first midget was a fellow by the name of Jerry D. Sullivan, who was often billed as "The Mighty Little Man" in addition to being an actor, acrobat, strongman, and gymnast. Sullivan was a favorite in vaudeville and burlesque circuits.

Here is Sullivan's story:

The 1905 season had been disappointing for the Buffalo, New York, Bisons. Under the management of George Stallings, they had won the pennant and the Junior World Series the previous year, but by September of 1905, it was clear that the team was stuck in fifth place and was not likely to come close to another pennant.

Stallings would later, in 1914, become the leader of the "Miracle Boston Braves," but for now he needed something to shake loose the devilment of loss and get his team back on track. Oddly enough, while he and his Bison team were staying in the city of Baltimore, Stallings met and struck up a friendship with a midget actor, named Jerry Sullivan, who was also living in the hotel during his engagement in a play called "Simple, Simon, Simple." He was playing the role of "Little Mose" in the musical which had recently opened in the Baltimore

The 17-Inch Baseball Bat

Academy of Music.

In a critique of the musical play, the Baltimore Sun had referred to it as, "a play of major importance with a large cast that included 50 lively chorus girls." It was a three hour extravaganza requiring no fewer than 287 elaborate costumes. The review brings to mind an old burlesque joke about "50 beautiful girls and 49 beautiful costumes," but that's another story.

It's been reported that Stallings had two separate personalities. One was a gentlemanly, Southern country squire when he was anywhere except on a baseball field. Apparently, something happened to Stallings' personality when he set foot on a baseball diamond and he became the devil incarnate. Baseball turned him into a hot-tempered, angry, profane, superstitious, and unpredictable personage. It's not a hard story to believe, of course, just look at what happens to some docile baseball fans when they click through the turnstile into a ballpark.

On September 18, per instructions from Stallings, little Jerry Sullivan arrived at Oriole Park all decked out in a Buffalo Bison uniform as the new "mascot" of the baseball team. By the start of the ninth inning, the Bisons trailed the Oriole team 10-2.

Opening the inning, catcher Frank McManus singled, bringing pitcher Stan Yerkes on deck and ready to bat. But Yerkes never had the chance to raise his bat.

He was intercepted by Sullivan, who was es-

The 17-Inch Baseball Bat

corted by Rube Kisinger, the resident clown and good-humor man of the Bison team. When Kisinger told the umpire, Charley Simmer, that Sullivan would be pinch-hitting for Yerkes, there wasn't the slightest glimmer of objection from Oriole manager Hugh Jennings, and the arbiter announced in a grave tone, "Sullivan batting for Yerkes." The fans were enthralled and they cheered the upcoming batter, as they are always expected to do.

Pitcher Fred Burchell of the Orioles was doubled over, laughing himself silly. He finally took some deep breathers, regained some composure, and launched the "dead ball" spheroid toward the plate. The first pitch was understandably quite high—ball one. His next pitch was better, being no more than six inches off the ground. And then the miracle occurred.

To everyone's utter amazement, the "Mightly Little Man" swung his bat with power and grace, connecting quite nicely with the ball, and it lofted easily over and beyond the head of the third baseman Charley Loudenslager. Surprising everyone, Sullivan ran quickly and efficiently to first base and was safely on. It became apparent that Sullivan was, as his sobriquet implied, an accomplished athlete and formidable foe.

Embarrassed, Burchell tried to pick Sullivan off at first base, but the little man scurried safely back. To further embarrass the pitcher, he laughed at him as he poked his head between

The 17-Inch Baseball Bat

the legs of first baseman Tim Jordan, who was 6-foot, 1-inch tall, almost twice as tall as Sullivan.

Next up, Jake Gettman singled, sending Sullivan on to second base. By this time, pitcher Burcell was both angry and agitated at this turn of events. His next pitch went five feet over the catcher's head, allowing Sullivan to almost amble his way safely onto third base. It was no help to Burcell that Sullivan continued to heckle him.

Frank LaPorte then came to the plate and lobbed a ball out toward centerfield allowing Sullivan to run toward home plate. Even though he could have walked across quite safely, he chose to slide headfirst over the plate for maximum audience appeal. He stood up, dusted himself off, and doffed his cap to the tremendous ovation offered by the crowd. With perfect actor's timing, he slowly replaced his cap, bowed to the ovation, and walked toward the dugout, where he turned and bowed one final time to the approving crowd.

In the morning newspaper, the "Baltimore Sun," it was reported that: "Sullivan, the new acquisition, finished his first game leading the entire Eastern League. Though "Mose" made a valiant effort, he was unable to pull the Bisons out of the tall timber to which they had been driven by the chirping Orioles. The final score was Baltimore 10, Buffalo 6.

When the Bisons left town that day, Jerry

The 17-Inch Baseball Bat

Sullivan, however, stayed behind, opting to resume his more familiar role allowing him to cavort among those "50 lively chorus girls." It is unknown what the future held for the minuscule actor-turned-ballplayer, but the record for all time shows that he played for the Buffalo Bisons in a regular Eastern League game, got on base with a valid hit, scored a run, and batted a perfect 1.000.

BALTIM'E	AB	R	B	P	A	E	BUFFALO	AB	R	B	P	A	E
Neal, ss	5	3	3	1	6	0	Gettman, cf	5	2	3	3	0	0
Kelly, cf	5	3	3	2	0	0	McAlli'r	5	1	2	0	2	0
McAleese, rf	5	3	5	1	0	0	Dele'y, 1b,rf	5	0	3	9	1	0
Jordan, lb	4	1	3	10	0	0	Laporte, as	5	1	2	2	4	0
O'Hara, lf	3	0	1	1	0	0	Murphy, lb	1	0	0	5	0	0
Louden'r, 3b	4	0	1	0	4	0	Milligan, rf	2	0	1	0	0	0
Mullen, 2b	4	0	1	6	4	0	Miller, lf	5	0	1	2	0	0
Rvers, c	4	0	0	6	0	0	Nattress, 2b	5	0	1	0	3	0
Burchell, p	4	0	0	0	1	0	McManus, c4	1	2	3	0	0	
Total	38	10	17	27	15	0	Yerkes, p	3	0	0	0	4	0
							*Sullivan	1	1	1	0	0	0
							Total	41	6	16	24	14	0

Baltimore	4	3	0	3	0	0	0	0	x	—10
Buffalo	0	0	1	0	1	0	0	0	4	— 6

*Sullivan batted for Yerkes in ninth inning.

Two-base hits—Jordan 2, Milligan, Mullen, McAleese. Sacrifice hits—O'Hara, Jordan. Double plays—Neal, Mullen, Jordan 2. First on balls—Off Burchell 1. Hit by pitcher—By Burchell 1. Struck out—By Burchell 3. Yerkes 2. Wild pitch—Burchell. Left on bases—Baltimore 7, Buffalo 8. Time—1:40. Umpires—Zimmer, Moran.

The 17-Inch Baseball Bat

Jerry Sullivan was born as Jeremiah David Sullivan on August 12, 1873 in Low, Québec, a Canadian logging town founded by Irish immigrants. Jerry was given the same name as his twenty-year-old brother, who had drowned while floating logs down-river to a mill.

Although Jerry's head and torso had developed normally, at his birth, his parents were told that Jerry would probably never grow beyond the height of four-feet. Like many midgets, he was ridiculed and mocked by classmates but while presenting an oral assignment of a humorous verse, in the second grade, he realized his "performance" received a large amount of laughter and applause from his classmates.

Soon after his classroom recitation, Jerry's family moved to Wausau, Wisconsin and by the time he was a teenager, Jerry attempted to capitalize on his physical stature. One such venture involved goats and a small wagon.

Working for local Mathie Brewing Company, he became something of a celebrity, riding in an advertising wagon drawn by a brace of goats. A double-sided placard promoted the brewers new "Bock Beer" which was a strong German ale enjoyed immensely by the local Wisconsinites.

Jerry had proven himself to be athletic in spite of his physique so he left home, joined the Robinson Family Circus, and learned all he

The 17-Inch Baseball Bat

could about being an acrobat and contortionist.

Branching out, he became involved with a traveling medicine show called Hamlin's Wizard Oil, which would have been useless except for the fact it was about 50-percent alcohol. During performances, Jerry would extoll the virtues of the company's "cure all elixir" in addition to imbibing a substantial quantity of it on-stage.

It was during his employment with Wizard Oil that Jerry became involved with professional baseball. When he had free time from the medicine show, he would exploit his abilities by appearing as an "added attraction" during baseball games, much like Max Patkin did during his career as The Clown Prince of Baseball.

In 1892 the Carroll, Iowa town team drafted the multi-talented Jerry to play against a Female Baseball Team from Denver, Colorado.

As can be imagined, Jerry stole the show, managing to hit a double while serving as the Carroll team's catcher. The local newspaper reported that, "Jerry's performance behind home plate was nothing less than wonderful. Little Jerry is a splendid curiosity and to watch him play baseball is worth the entire cost of a ticket."

During a Wizard Oil troupe visit to Missoula, Montana, Jerry offered to umpire a re-match between Missoula's town team and the nearby Anaconda's town team.

In spite of Missoula's sound thrashing of the Anacondas—a severe 26-to-2 victory—even the losing team solidly praised Jerry as, " . . . the

The 17-Inch Baseball Bat

best umpire that has officiated the grounds this season. He also proved to be an entire circus just by himself."

Anaconda was so impressed with Jerry they invited him to join them the following week as one of their players. An Anaconda spokesman said, "He can catch, he can throw, and he can most certainly hit with the best of them. Nor is he any kind of a slouch when running the bases."

Tiring of the medicine show game, Jerry quit in 1899 and made his way into the vaudeville circuit, joining a popular tumbling act and impressing audiences with great exploits of athleticism. He added a comedy bit to the act in which he played the part of a wrestler.

His antics were noticed by a named Gus Hill who was a nationally known entertainer and a juggler of Indian clubs. Gus was tired of "treading the boards" so he became a manager, building his own cadre of speciality acts for the vaudeville circuit.

His first venture was a traveling company called the "Royal Lilliputians" and from what he had seen in the acrobat act, Gus figured that Jerry was just the midget he was looking for. Jerry's eyes lit up when he heard Gus' offer and he signed a contract in a New York minute.

His main part of the act, at first, was to drive a miniature fire engine across the stage which was pulled by a large goat. He certainly had the credentials for such a performance after his ini-

The 17-Inch Baseball Bat

tial foray into the entertainment industry as an advertiser for the Mathie Brewing Company.

Gus' next venture, a vaudeville farce, was called "McFadden's Row of Flats." It was based on the Yellow Kid Comic Strip and Gus figured that Jerry would be perfect as the human personification of the Yellow Kid, himself.

Following those two successes, Gus put Jerry into his national touring company of a show called "Simple Simon Simple." Jerry played a character named Mose, who made his appearance by popping out of a laundry basket. Jerry was an instant hit and he delighted audiences everywhere.

In 1901, Jerry met and married a normal-sized gal named Helen "Nellie" Bates. She was one of the many chorus girls in the "Simple Simon Simple" show. They were married on the day before Valentine's Day much to the chagrin of Nellie's father who had discouraged Nellie's show business ambitions. He thought even less of her marrying Jerry. He said, "About a week ago, I heard my daughter had married this dwarf. I was surprised, as any father would be, at such dismal news. But, she's a grown woman and she's old enough to know what she's doing so I made no attempt to prevent it."

Nellie, who was 5-feet, 4-inches tall, once said laughingly, "He's mighty little for a husband, but I think it will be nice to have a husband I can pick up and shake when I feel like it."

The 17-Inch Baseball Bat

After the wedding, Jerry kept busy at his chosen profession and his travels took him back and forth across the country for the next several years.

It was in 1905, during Jerry's involvement with "Simple Simon Simple" that his famous baseball game occurred—as is fully explained in this book.

In spite of his 1,000 batting average, a walk on balls, and a scoring run, Jerry decided that professional baseball really wasn't the way to make a living. Six weeks later, he was in New York City, portraying his Mose character in Broadway's "West End Theater." Jerry had made it into the "big leagues" of the musical stage.

During the summer of 1907, Jerry ignored a deadly heat wave in Philadelphia, Pennsylvania, to attend the National Elks Convention. It was no surprise when he was awarded the title of "Littlest Elk." He earned a cash prize and he had the honor of leading a massive parade through the city streets. Accompanying him on the head of the parade, was another Elk who carried the title of the "Tallest Elk."

In 1907, a young man named Bud Fisher launched a new newspaper comic strip named "Mutt & Jeff" which was an instant success. When King Features syndicated the comic strip nationwide, it made Bud Fisher a very wealthy man and it changed Jerry Sullivan's life.

It was so popular, in fact, that Gus Hill obtained the rights to use the two characters in an

The 17-Inch Baseball Bat

on-going series of musical theater performances that toured the vaudeville circuit. At one time, Gus had a total of six touring companies on the road simultaneously. His "Mutt & Jeff" franchise of musical extravaganzas made him an extremely wealthy man.

Unfortunately, Jerry wasn't the best of businessmen and he signed a bad contract. He ended up playing the midget "Jeff" throughout North America for almost twenty years and for his trouble he was paid minimum scale. When the run of "Mutt & Jeff" ended, he was no better off then when he had started.

When Jerry was in either New York or Los Angeles, during off hours from the stage, he was able to pull in some extra cash by performing in silent movies but he never made a name for himself in that segment of the entertainment industry. Unfortunately, the few movies in which he appeared have all disappeared; most probably destroyed. The old celluloid type of film had a habit of turning to dust in the can.

When the film, "The Court Jester" played in Jerry's hometown, the local newspaper beat the drum loudly, saying, "Come and See Jerry Sullivan—a Wausau Boy!"

"Moving Picture World" magazine said in a brief review of the movie, "In this film the dwarf who made such a favorable impression in the fairy-story "The Little Old Men of the Woods" plays a prominent part, and he does it, if anything, better than he performed his earlier task."

The 17-Inch Baseball Bat

Commenting on his "film work" Jerry said, "No matter how immortal a person is made by film, no matter what stage of perfection motion pictures reach, a play by living people will always be the principal source of amusement."

It was more bad news for Jerry when sound was added to films. As sound motion-picture quality increased, there came a decline in the popularity of vaudeville and almost all of Jerry's employment venues ceased to exist.

Jerry briefly returned to the circus in 1929, but it was much too strenuous for the little guy. For a guy born in 1873, the vaudeville circuit, and all its traveling, was a hard life.

His next job was with two other midgets working an act at "Wonderland" on Coney Island, near the amusement parks where he could sometimes find odd jobs. The next job he found was working in a side-show with the billing of "Jerry—The Dwarf!"

During this period of his life, Jerry began the habit of frequenting the bar at the "Circus Room" of the Cumberland Hotel in New York City. One can easily imagine how his life went following that.

In September of 1937, Jerry was placed under arrest after standing on a street corner and drunkenly heckling a dozen or so members of the American Legion, shouting at them, "You're all phonies. You've never been across the seas. I could lick every one of you."

Although the Legionnaires laughed it off, a

The 17-Inch Baseball Bat

nearby police officer heard Jerry and told him to mind his own business before he got himself hurt.

Jerry turned on the police officer, challenged and threatened him, and the next thing Jerry knew, he was cooling his heels in the local drunk tank.

The following morning, a magistrate called Jerry before him and Jerry gave the judge a military salute, pleaded guilty, and admitted that he had, indeed, been drunk the night before. He said, "I'm all right now, though, judge."

The judge asked, "Will you be a good boy from now on?"

64-year-old Jerry replied very solemnly to his honor that he would certainly be a good boy and the judge gave him a suspended sentence.

In December, 1940, Jerry was mentioned in a very short newspaper notice that he had been in attendance at the funeral of five-hundred-pound "Jolly Irene." Irene was a former Barnum & Bailey side-show performer who had worked with Jerry at Coney Island.

Jerry's marriage to Nellie was finished by this time, too. In the 1940 census, Jerry was listed as being married, but living alone. That census record is the final known iteration of Jerry Sullivan's existence.

It's often sad the way time and life take a toll on people and Jerry was no exception. Forgotten are the things he accomplished, the way he made people laugh, and that day when he was a

The 17-Inch Baseball Bat

professional baseball player for an afternoon. A player with a hit, a walk, and a scoring run. A player with a batting average of 1,000.

The 17-Inch Baseball Bat

George Stallings; manager of the Buffalo Bisons professional baseball team, 1905.

The 17-Inch Baseball Bat

Jerry Sullivan as a teenager. Decked out in a new suit and ready for his first job interview.

The 17-Inch Baseball Bat

Having gotten himself hired by the Mathie Brewing Co., Jerry Sullivan retains his dapper accoutrements while traveling around town informing the populace that Mathie Bock Beer will be "on tap" tomorrow, per the placard.

The 17-Inch Baseball Bat

Jerry Sullivan in one of his first theatrical roles.
On the right, he's the "half pint" character Jeff
in this production called "Mutt & Jeff."

The 17-Inch Baseball Bat

Jerry D. Sullivan, 1905.

The 17-Inch Baseball Bat

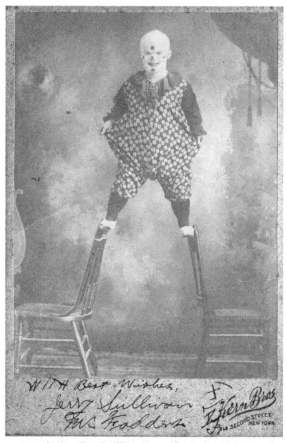

Jerry D. Sullivan performing his
ever popular acrobat routine.

The 17-Inch Baseball Bat

Jerry Sullivan, in costume as "Little Mose" for the 1905 musical extravaganza, "Simple, Simon, Simple."

The 17-Inch Baseball Bat

Larry Tattersall

The second midget ballplayer who must be included here is a fellow by the name of Larry Tattersall, at least that's his real moniker and the one he used as a ballplayer in 1948.

Unable to make a career of professional baseball as a midget, Larry departed the baseball diamond and headed for the professional wrestling ring—or should it be called the "rasslin' ring?"

Changing his name to "Sonny Boy" Cassidy, he spent most of his professional rasslin' career in St. Louis, Missouri performing at the Chase Park Plaza Hotel—the same place that Gorgeous George made a name for himself by throwing gold-plated hairpins to the audience. I hate to admit this, but my Aunt Theresa watched these matches religiously on television and was very often in the live audience at the hotel, too.

What's the deal with St. Louis? It's the city of the Squawks team in Thurber's story, it's where Gaedel played for the Browns, and it's where Sonny Boy Cassidy was a professional "rassler." It makes me wonder. For what it's worth, here's the Tattersall (Cassidy) story:

The 17-Inch Baseball Bat

In 1948, Larry "Tat" Tattersall was hailed as the smallest pinch-hitter on the globe after he helped win a game for North Providence High School in Rhode Island. This occurred three years before Eddie Gaedel burst into the big league scene.

In spite of his diminutive size, Tat proved to be a natural athlete who played hockey, basketball, and baseball for his high school.

Tat was warming the bench that day in 1948 when North Providence loaded the bases against Woonsocket in the last of the ninth with the score tied, two out, and a weak hitter due at the plate.

Dick Flynn, the North Providence coach, waggled a finger at Tat, who hopped down from the bench, picked up a bat approximately as long as himself, and listened carefully to the coach's instructions.

"You're on your own," said Flynn, "but keep away from that umpire. He's so blind he'll trample you to death."

The umpire was Hank Soar, who later became an American League umpire. He had left the NY Giants football team and was coaching the Rhode Island State College backfield while trying to break into professional baseball.

When Soar saw Tattersall walk up to the plate, he said, "Get behind the backstop, kid. You'll get killed out here."

With awe-inspiring confidence, Tat looked at Soar and proclaimed, "I'm the hitter."

The 17-Inch Baseball Bat

Soar wheeled around to bellow toward the North Providence bench, "Get this kid outta here, Flynn. He's too low for an umpire."

"Don't be silly, Albert Henry," Flynn said. "There's nothing too low for an umpire."

Soar shrugged his shoulders and indicated to Tat that he could enter the batter's box.

The Woonsocket pitcher did his best, but the first three deliveries were too high for Tat's small-scale strike zone.

Gus Savaria, Woonsocket's coach, called time out. Gus was a solid baseball man, justly respected for sending Clem Labine to the big leagues.

Savaria spoke to his catcher, "Kneel down," he said, "and give him a target." The catcher knelt, and the pitcher got two strikes over. The count was three and two when Flynn called time..

"Go into a crouch," coach Flynn told Tattersall.

"Lie down and give him a target," Savaria told the Woonsocket catcher.

Everybody gave it his best Sunday try, but the Woonsocket pitcher missed the strike zone. Hank Soar said, "Ball four," and the winning run crossed the plate for North Providence.

The next day's sports section of the newspaper said, "Everybody in the littlest state is still mighty proud of the littlest athlete who has converted his handicap into an asset."

In 1952, using the alias of Sonny Boy Cas-

The 17-Inch Baseball Bat

sidy, Tat won the Midget Wrestling World Championship at the St. Louis Chase Park Plaza Hotel, taking two-out-of-three falls against Farmer Pete, the Hillbilly 'Rassler.

It was reported that over six thousand people were in attendance to see Tat's thumping of Farmer Pete.

The 17-Inch Baseball Bat

Larry Tattersall (Sonny Boy Cassidy) is on the left, squaring off against Farmer Pete for the Midget Wrestler Championship in 1952. Below, "Tat" has just applied a knee to the head of Farmer Pete.

The 17-Inch Baseball Bat

Larry Tattersall (aka Sonny Boy Cassidy) as he appeared in 1968, nearing the end of his professional wrestling career.

The 17-Inch Baseball Bat

Edmond Ansley, the first midget to assume the character of "Buster Brown" was the spokesman for the shoe company for 27 years. He died of a heart attack in Gainesville, Texas on September 28, 1972 at the age of 84. His measured height was 4-foot, 2-inches tall.

The 17-Inch Baseball Bat

Perhaps the most famous of American midgets was Billy Barty, (born William John Bertanzetti, on October 25, 1924). He began his career working with Mickey Rooney in silent movies. He made over sixty films, appeared in countless television shows, created the "Little People of America" organization and he preferred the term "Little People" instead of "midgets." He specialized in roles as a wise-cracker and during the 1950s, he was a regular on the Spike Jones Show. His career spanned seven decades.

The 17-Inch Baseball Bat

Johnny Roventini was the most successful midget of them all. Standing 4-feet, 11-inches tall, he was the human advertising logo for Philip Morris cigarettes for most of his life. His contract provided him with $20,000 a year and an automobile for life. His "Bell Hop" call was as famous as he was: "Caaaal Fooor Philip Morrrisss." He even changed his legal name to Johnny Philip Morris.

The 17-Inch Baseball Bat

During the 1950s, actor Max Bournstein assumed the character of "Mr. Zero" to promote the Zero Candy Bar made by the Hollywood Candy Company. The Zero bar had a special coating that kept it from melting in warm temperatures. The bars were sold for 3-cents, which undercut the 5-cent Hershey bar by a full two pennies. Two pennies were a lot of money to a little kid in those days. "Mr. Zero" toured the United States in a "Crosley Super-Sport" with the Zero Logo painted on both sides.

Made in the USA
Monee, IL
15 June 2025

19444857R00115